MW00328731

Run. Think. Repeat.

Funny, thought-provoking and totally
random thoughts from a mom on the run

Run. Think. Repeat.
Copyright © 2017 Kim Rezendes. All rights reserved.

This is a work of fiction. Names, characters, places and incidents are products of the author's imagination or are used fictitiously and should not be construed as real. Any resemblance to actual events, locales, organizations or persons, living or dead, is entirely coincidental.

No part of this book may be used or reproduced in any manner whatsoever without written permission, except in the case of brief quotations embodied in critical articles and reviews. For more information, e-mail all inquiries to info@mindstirmedia.com.

Published by Mindstir Media LLC
45 Lafayette Rd. Suite 181 | North Hampton, NH 03862 | USA
1.800.767.0531 | www.mindstirmedia.com

Printed in the United States of America
ISBN-13: 978-0-9986975-5-0
Library of Congress Control Number: 2017908806

RUN. THINK. REPEAT.

FUNNY, THOUGHT-PROVOKING AND TOTALLY RANDOM THOUGHTS FROM A MOM ON THE RUN

The way I see it, life is like a morning run. Some days, you start out fierce, set the pace, and you stay strong until the end. You finish and you're ready for the next go-round tomorrow. Other days, even tying your running shoes is a battle. You trip on your way out the door, you get chased by your neighbor's dog and it starts to pour as you turn the first corner.

But either way, you did it. You finished the run. Don't you feel better?

I love to run. I really do.

Running gives me time to think - really think - about this thing we call life.
It isn't always perfect.
But at least as far as I can see, it's the only life I've got.
So I say, embrace it, love it, live it. And while you're at it, enjoy.

MINDSTIR MEDIA

KIM'S NOTE:

So, here's my "for what it's worth" advice before you jump in to reading this book, which has been loosely organized in to four types of stories:

FamiLove – stories about family, friends and every-day life in this crazy messed-up go-round.

"Her"story – stories that were dusted off as they went from in my head to in this book as they are old and surely forgotten (or even unknown) by some.

"RanDumbs" – yep, you guessed it. I don't pretend to think about heavy, earth-shattering stuff all the time (or ever), so stories show you how my brain works. As scary as that is.

Think, Thank, Thunk – stories that are interspersed with other "fluffier" ones that may not necessarily be for the faint of heart. If these don't tug at your heart strings, brains, and/or emotions, you may want to check your pulse and get back to me in the morning.

You know when you run (or pretty much do anything), how your mind takes you all over the place? You think a little bit about this and then a little bit about that. Then you go back to this and then fixate on that again for a while. My mind works like that, (but on overdrive), when I run. And so, the stories in this book all were born in my head at some point while I was running. They will take you all over the place, from "happy" to "sad" to "emotional" to "this Kim chick is nuts, her husband needs a medal."

So, if you don't like the chapter you're reading, don't worry. There's a new one just around the corner and you'll be able to forget about the one you're on before you turn the page. (But don't forget about it too much. You need to tell your friends...and tell them to buy this book...I have two kids to put through college!)

Enjoy!

*To Guy – for your humor, lack of patience and love of all things family, friends and football. You were the boy on the bus that teased me. You'll also be the boy growing old with me. I am blessed beyond measure that you are mine.

*To Hannah and Madison/Madison and Hannah – for helping me cherish (nearly) every minute of this journey that we are on together. I've lived more years without you than I have with you, but I can't imagine how I got through a single moment until I learned that you both were our reality. You both make our Four Family shine bright.

*To my parents – for rocking the universe with your eternal awesomeness.

*To my "every day" friends and family– for putting up with me on a regular basis. You each deserve a medal. Having you as a part of my village makes so many things, for me, possible.

*To my "new" friends - I have been known to often say that I don't have time for or need "new" friends. I'm glad that I was wrong when it comes to you.

*To my "forever" friends – thank you for being my lifeline. Always.

*To my family – you are my blessings. Each and every one of you. Well, except some of you. Some of you are just plain weird...

*To my Usher Dupey, Gram, Auntie Maffie, Uncle Louie, Auntie Ellie, Uncle Freddie and Auntie Jan – you never had a chance to see me run. But you are with me every step of the way, and you are the ones that meet me first at every finish line.

Kim does not consider herself a writer.

Nor does she consider herself a runner.

And yet, she has written a book compiled of thoughts that she had while running.

Go figure.

An Assistant Director at the Franklin School for the Performing Arts, she serves as Director of LITTLE MUSIC SCHOOL and Instructor of Musical Theater. Her classes are 50% educational and 50% comical as she tries to maneuver her way around a classroom filled with 1-9 year olds each week. (Not for the faint of heart.) She wishes she had super cool hobbies, like visiting the Seven Wonders of the World or hang gliding across the Pacific, but really she enjoys cooking, spending as much time as she can at the Cape with her family and friends, and loving her two daughters and husband with a fierceness that she never imagined. They reside in Franklin, Massachusetts (where she has lived her whole life), and it is where she will stay until her husband has had enough of shoveling New England snow and they move south. (Well, at least for part of the year. You can take the girl out of Boston but you can't take Boston out of the girl.)

THOUGHTS

Running. Why do we do it?

As I gear up for another long run tomorrow, it still makes me laugh that I do this at all. I do not consider myself a runner. Really. I am someone who runs. There's a very big difference.

I never ran a day in my life until 2001. I had a lot going on back then and I needed to do something to keep my mind occupied while it felt as if my life was crumbling around me. So, I started to run. Literally, yards at a time. I was very patient and, little by little, the mileage added up.

The first race I ever ran was a 5K. I was, no joke, the last person over the finish line. I had no idea how to pace myself. I started way in front (I always sat in the front of the bus and in front of the classroom. Wasn't it the same?!) I didn't even know how to pin on my number. Clueless. My dad cheered me on as if I were running (and winning) the Boston Marathon. Best. Dad. Ever.

The more I ran, the more I enjoyed it and the better I became at it. Over time, I ran a few 10Ks and such and, with some words of wisdom from one of my best buds since junior high, I kept upping the ante. Love you, Mel!

Seemingly out of nowhere, a few years ago, I decided that I wanted to run a marathon before I turned forty. I have no idea why that suddenly became so important to me. Most people in my world thought I was nuts. I've now run two full marathons and I'm getting antsy to do another one.

I still run a bunch now. And I love it.

So, why do I run?

I run -
Because I can.
Because I love running for hours when I can either think of a ton of stuff or nothing at all.
Because I think it's important for Maddie and Hannah to see me take some time out for me.
Because Hannah and Maddie now run short distances with me. Guy does, sometimes, too.

Because, if I didn't run, I'd be at least twenty pounds heavier. At least. (Have I mentioned I love to eat?)

Because it has helped me appreciate these four crazy seasons in this neck of the woods. It's like an entirely different sport, depending on the season.

Because it gives me hours throughout the week when I can be by myself. As much as I love the peeps in my life, I love being without the peeps in my life too.

Because I am way proud of myself for doing something as crazy as running 26.2 miles – twice. I never thought I'd be able to do that. High five, me!

That's me, just yards away from finishing my first marathon in October, 2010. I'm pretty sure that I was saying to my family, "Holy SHIT! I just DID this!" My time was just over four hours. What?

#1 Day of my Life: The day Hannah and Maddie were born.

#2 Day of my Life: Our Wedding.

#3 and #4 Days of my Life: the first time and then the second time I ran 26.2 miles. I can honestly say I enjoyed every minute.

No question. Best days ever.

So tomorrow, I plan on running 13.1 miles. I was supposed to run a formal half in Hyannis but the weather is going to be gross and, while I don't mind running in it, I hate the idea of driving in it. (As odd as that sounds, that logic makes perfect sense to me…)

So, I will run that distance. And then I will come home. And eat. A lot. Because that's what I do.

A LOVE STORY

Perhaps I'm feeling a bit romantic. Please indulge me as I share this story of true love.

Before Guy and I got married, we attended a day-long Pre-Cana class. (For you non-Catholics, this is a fancy way of saying a mandatory day of marriage counseling. Because priests know a lot about being married.)

At one point in the day, we were all instructed to write a letter to our future spouses. It was a long time ago, but to the best of my recollection, the letter was supposed to express what we loved about the other person, what we most looked forward to as husband and wife, you know that type of thing. It was pretty much a love letter...that a priest told us to write...I guess that's weird. But whatever. We did what we were told. We were blinded by love.

I, of course, took this assignment very seriously. I don't remember what I wrote but I labored over this letter. I wanted to share with Guy all that was in my heart and soul. I was so in love with him. I couldn't wait to proclaim our love in front of family and friends. I couldn't believe that I had found the love of my life in him, someone I'd known all along.

As I was writing my letter, I watched Guy put pen to paper. He was very busy writing. He never looked up from his paper. I was intrigued as he's not typically one to gush over anything (well, except the Patriots but, much to his dismay, he wasn't marrying the Patriots.) Seeing how seriously he was taking this was making me fall in love with him all over again.

I finished my letter and anxiously waited to read his.

Well, this is what he wrote. No joke.

"Dear Kim,

I really love you.

Love, Guy"

I should have known, then and there, what I was getting myself into.

I have no one to blame but myself. And I do. Daily.

REALITY

Maddie and Hannah have just finished their first week back to school. Everything went great. As to be expected. Phew! You never know how re-entry is going to be after a long summer of fun in the sun.

Even though I work all summer, I am very spoiled that they can hang with me in or around my office. (Have I mentioned that I love my job?) But because of this, the first few weeks of fall are always a bit of a culture shock for me. We are together all summer and then, BAM! They are gone.

I miss them. My office is strangely quiet.

Tonight, we will head down the Cape as soon as they finish up class. Yes, please.

I can't wait to chat and get all the deets about their new year. I can't wait to have some un-interrupted time with them.

Until they start bugging me and I turn up the radio so I can't hear them anymore.

JUST A GLIMPSE

Dear Gram,

To say that your legacy lives on in me, my cousins and our children is an understatement. We are all more like you than we even realize sometimes. (Much to the dismay, I'm sure, of our spouses…)

We joke that you called me "a miracle" to everyone (who'd pretend to listen). Your pride in me and the rest of your grandchildren and great-grandchildren went unmatched. I beg anyone to challenge me on that truth.

You never missed a single "Kim's First Day of School". Ever. Even when I was in college, you'd head up to our house to say goodbye before we headed south on 495. At the time, I just sort of expected that you'd do it, because you had always done it. I would have completely understood if you ever weren't able to, but it would have been weird. Now, looking back, I am in awe of it. What a simple, quick visit can do for a kid…

I can't think of a single "thing" of mine that you missed – recitals, shows, presentations, parties, meetings, you name it – you were there. In fact, when Hannah and Maddie were little and we enrolled them in their first music/movement/run around like crazy kids-class, I didn't want to take them by myself so who came with me each week? You, of course.

While I would sing in church, you would tell every single person who walked by you that I was your granddaughter (and a lot of people walked by you because you were sitting in your fifth row pew 30-minutes before mass started each week). Yes, Gram – they thought I was beautiful. Yes, Gram – they thought I sounded amazing. And yes, Gram – they knew that I was a miracle. You had already told them that for the past 10,794 Sundays.

Your ability to not take things too seriously (including yourself) is a quality that I am proud to say I see in myself. Like you, I let most things roll off my back. And like you, if I do get upset about something, look out. I mean business.

Every time I need something to be hemmed or mended, my first thought is to "give it to Gram." That's one thing that I did NOT get from you. I cannot even thread a needle successfully but that's okay. You taught me lots of other things.

Most of the phrases that I have coined as mine are really not mine at all. They are yours. I share them with you. And I melt a little each time I hear Maddie and Hannah saying them too.

But, Gram, I am angry about one thing. And it's a pretty big thing actually. Don't worry. It's not your fault. Not at all. It's not anyone's fault, which is part of the problem. There's no one to blame.

Gram, you were taken from us way too early. For a few years, "you" were with us but "You" weren't. It started innocently enough and, because we didn't know what was going on, when you said or did something that didn't make sense, we all just thought "Oh, that's just 'Gram being Gram'". Soon enough, though, that didn't cut it any more. We knew that you were leaving us. It happened slowly at first and then, as if in a blink, "You" were gone. Suddenly, we didn't know you anymore. You looked like you. You sounded like you (most of the time). But you weren't you. We lost you and we didn't have a map to get you back home to us again.

As I walked down the hallway to visit you, I would pray, "Please, God, please let me catch a glimpse of Gram today. Please, God, let her say something that'll be 'just like her' today. Please let her recognize and remember me and why I'm visiting. Please, God, let her completely understand everything I am saying to her."

Some days, at the beginning, my prayers would be answered. I'd catch a glimpse of you. And I'd be so happy. Like a little kid. I had you back. But as time went on, these glimpses got fewer and fewer.

It just didn't make sense. In my head, I would shout, "What do you mean you don't know this, that or the other? You're my Gram, dammit! How can you not know what I'm talking about?!!" Then, I'd get in my car and I'd cry. You know, the big, from the depths of your soul cry.

I'd go back the next day for our next visit, and pray for another glimpse. And I did that until the very last day.

I miss you, Gram. I would say, "I miss you more than you know." But the amazing thing is, Gram, that I believe that you do know. I believe that you now know every breath that I have taken and will ever take. Now you understand everything – everything that has ever happened and everything that will ever happen to me.

You have more than a glimpse of me. You have an eternity.

ODE TO THE DRINK

Oh, how I miss thee.
Your bubbles.
Your straw.
Your perfect ice to liquid ratio.
(You can't get it "just right" anywhere else.)

The cup holder in my car is empty.
I wait for you.
I miss you.
 I know that you will be back but not soon enough.
(Easter Sunday seems like a lifetime away.)

After dinner last night, I was sad. So very, very sad.
I had some juice.
I had some water.
Nothing.
Nothing helped.
(If I resort to drinking the only other beverage that I really like – wine – I will
have bigger headaches than those brought on by the caffeine withdrawal.)
So I went to bed thirsty.
And I dreamed of you.

You may know this already, but we are so close, you and I.
You complete me.
I swear, I'm going to be dehydrated from my run tomorrow.
(Most people drink water after a run. I'm not like most people.)

There is no substitute for you.
I am in love with you.
I miss you.

And I will continue to miss you.
Until we meet again, fountain machine Diet Coke.

Until we meet again.

THE CLEANSING

I was in eighth grade. My parents surprised me, my grandparents, my Auntie Ellie and my Auntie Maffie, with a trip to Italy. It was an amaaaaazing trip of a lifetime, visiting family and seeing "the old country." I think I appreciated it as much as I could at the time and now, as an adult, I appreciate it even more.

One day, we visited our "rich" cousins (and I say that because they had Atari and indoor plumbing...). My parents and the rest of my immediate family went out for the night with my cousins. I stayed home with my cousin, Angela Marie. When I was a kid, (not unlike other kids), my concept of adults' ages was admittedly skewed. So, I have no idea how old Angela Marie was. At the time, I thought that she was probably mid-70's. Looking back on it now, I bet (no joke) that she was late 30's.

Angela Marie and I were home in their apartment. She was a cute, little, lovely lady who smelled like garlic and Ivory soap, in that order. She didn't speak a word of English and I, sadly, spoke no Italian. (I don't have many regrets in life, but not asking my family to teach me how to speak Italian is one of them.) I know it's not too late to learn, but I really wish I could have learned from them.

I don't remember much of the night. But, at some point, I understood that she asked me if I wanted to take a bath. "Sure," I said in my eighth-grade head. It was August in Italy. I'm sure I smelled like, well, Italy in August.

There was a claw-foot tub. There were bubbles. There was the smell of homemade sauce coming in from the kitchen. And suddenly, there was Angela Marie. In the bathroom. Totally bathing me.

It happened so quickly. I know it sounds ridiculous but there was truly no way to stop it.

Now, please. She was not in the LEAST bit bathing me in a creepy "my cousin is attacking me-no one will believe me-she is preying on my naiveté" way. She was bathing me in a "you are my cousin from America-I want to take care of you-I can't tell you how much I love you because you are a stupid American who only speaks one language-so let me show you how much I love you" kind of way. (Well, that still sounds weird, but it really wasn't.)

Well, wait. It WAS weird. I was 13. Everything is weird when you're 13. I was totally and completely dying inside but, at the same time, I knew that she meant nothing other than expressing her complete and total love to me. (Well, that sounds weird too… but it really wasn't…well it was, but…)

So, fast forward. The "longest bath in the history of baths" ended, my family came home, and I kicked their Italian asses in centipede. I'm not even sure how or when I even told my family about the bath incident.

I wish you could have seen my face during The Cleansing.
I wish I could have seen my face during The Cleansing.
Classic.

PTSD

Today, in my world, PTSD stands for Post Traumatic Swim Disorder.

My parents (because they rock the world), took the kids for an overnight to Coco Keys last night. Guy and I had a great night – we did some shopping, had a quiet dinner outside at a cute little restaurant and then spent the rest of the night with great friends. (While at dinner, he said something that was so funny, I spit my wine out on the floor. That sort of laugh makes me so happy. I'm not so sure our waitress agreed as she was cleaning up after me.)

Anyhow, on the way home earlier today, Hannah had a horrible allergic reaction to something. She was miserable. Hives and a rash all over. Poor babe.

I don't know what made me sadder – seeing Hannah so miserable or seeing Maddie so miserable because Hannah was so miserable.

It's like something you can't even imagine, this connection these two have.

A few days ago, they both happened to fall asleep for a few minutes on the couch. They spent a minute or so, talking back and forth in some sort of crazy twin gibberish. It was not unlike what we have witnessed a number of times. We have caught them a few times in the middle of the night, clearly having a sound-asleep conversation with each other, complete with gibberish questions, answers and giggles.

When they were three or so, Hannah was on the couch with Guy. Maddie was upstairs taking a nap. Suddenly, in her barely-even-able-to-speak-yet-sort-of-way, Hannah turned to Guy and said, "Sister up". Guy hadn't heard a thing. Sure enough, he walked over to the steps and just as he was doing so, Maddie turned the corner and came out of their bedroom from her nap. There was NO WAY that Hannah could have seen or heard Maddie. She just KNEW that she was awake. To this day, Guy says that it was one of the coolest things he's ever seen.

Watching Maddie try to make Hannah feel better today made my heart literally hurt. Soon enough I had two crying kids. They were not being overly dramatic, trying to get a reaction from us. They just can't stand to see each other sick, hurt or upset. (Unless, of course, one is the direct source of the pain aka kicking, pulling hair, poking in the ribs – you know, regular sister stuff.)

It's way cool, this life they lead. And as I've said many times before, I'm so happy to have a front row seat for the show!

JUST BREATHE

The girls frequently ask what Heaven is like.

We tell them what we THINK Heaven is like but that we obviously are not even remotely experts on the subject – not yet anyway.

Last night, Hannah asked me if I think that you can smell your "home smell" in Heaven.

My answer was a resounding "yes" because to me, Heaven is your own version of Perfection. It is filled with all that you love. In my Heaven, you taste, smell, spend time with, see, and feel your own version of Perfection. (And, apparently, to Hannah, her "home smell" is my red sauce, by the way, but I digress.)

This weekend, I talked with a guy who is, well to say he's a dear, dear friend is an understatement. I mean this guy has no idea what he means to us. Anyway, somehow, we got on the subject of Heaven.

He told me that his version of Heaven is Nine Minutes.

Nine Minutes.

The time between when you hit "snooze" and the next time your alarm goes off.

He thinks Heaven feels like these nine minutes.

It's the start of a new day.

Whatever was wrong the day before is over. It's done. You can't change it.

You can move on, learn from it and start a new day, full of potential (...in nine minutes...)

And yet, it's not quite the new day yet. (Remember? You still have nine minutes left.)

So anything you need to worry about, well, it can wait a few minutes longer. (You got it. Nine minutes longer...)

You don't need to talk. Or tell. Or ask. Or debate. Or remember. Or call. Or text. Or drive. (Don't ever do those last two things at the same time...) Or cook. Or pick up. Or build. Or clean. Or yell. Or annoy. Or be annoyed. Or cry. Or fire. Or hire. Or fix. Or. Or.

You only need to "be".

Nine minutes. It's the only time he gives himself, each day, to just be. To just Be.

BE.

And being is a great thing to be.

I think that we all should do it. For more than nine minutes. Because Heaven can wait.

02038

I ended up running 11 miles all alone this morning so I had a long time by myself to think. That's one of the reasons why I really like running alone. I don't often find myself alone for more than a few minutes most days, so running alone gives me a chance to shake out the cobwebs in my head and think about whatever I want.

Today, I thought about my hometown, good ol' Franklin, MA. It is where I have lived my entire life. I can't imagine living anywhere else. My parents grew up here. My husband grew up here. So did my grandparents and most of my cousins, aunts and uncles.

It is my home. It is our home.

I have a history here, decades and decades long. It doesn't let me forget where I came from or where I'm going. I'm pretty sure I'd have been a good kid anyway, but this town wouldn't let me be otherwise. I didn't want to let my family or the town down. I still feel this way.

When I was growing up, I never really said (out loud) that I wanted to stay in Franklin as an adult. I think I just always knew that I would. I'm not even sure if Guy and I officially talked about where we'd live once we were married. Living in Franklin was, I guess, a given. Phew.

I totally recognize that there are plenty of people who cannot WAIT to leave their hometown. I absolutely get that. The idea of living in the same town, practically on the same street, for your whole life, would surely suffocate many. I get it. But, quite honestly, I can't imagine not living here. I love to travel and if our bank account allowed, we'd travel more – as a couple and as a Four Family. I do sometimes think about packing up and leaving for someplace far away for a while – someplace entirely different from here. If our life allowed it, I really think I'd do it. I'd love to see more of the world and I'd love to see it with Guy and the girls. Then, when that stint was up, I'd happily come back to my hometown. Because it's where I belong.

As I ran this morning, I can't tell you how many people I knew as they drove past. Generations old family friends, students' parents, family members, friends, friends who are family – you get the point. It made me feel so deeply connected to this place. Of course, if I lived someplace else, I'd know plenty of people and feel amazing connections with them as well, connections not unlike what I have here perhaps. But, for me, I think I'd miss "this". This deep-rooted connection. I'd miss not having a history with so many

22

people that I bump into on a daily basis. I love that.

Surely I don't know where Hannah and Maddie will end up. If you ask them right now, they want to live in side-by-side houses, right next to our house. They want to go to school in Boston and go out for lunch with Guy and our dear friend, Poni, on a weekly basis.

Who knows if they will? But wherever they end up, I hope they never forget this town. This place where their roots have already been planted. Alongside the roots of so many others who love this town. Alongside the roots of so many others who love them. Alongside my roots. Their roots. Our roots.

Oh, Ward...

I frequently refer to myself as "June" because Guy, aka "Ward", takes care of most things. And quite simply, in our house, Ward takes care of most of these things because, well, because he is the boy.

I prefer not to talk to people who work at banks or insurance companies, appliance repair people or credit card companies.

Pretty much, unless it involves friends, family or food, I prefer to ignore it until it goes away (or until Guy is home to deal with it).

If he drops dead tomorrow, I am in big fat trouble because I don't know the first thing about running a household. But I can make a delicious red sauce and homemade garlic bread.

Well, this morning after her run, June was very, very busy doing things that Ward usually does because Ward is away.

And June is very tired from doing all of these things.

June needs a drink.

TMM

"TMM" = "The Miracle Mom".

My mom was in a pretty serious boating accident a few years ago. There are so many ridiculous things to say about this. I don't know where to start. We were never "boat people" and surely this whole event sealed the deal. The long and the short of it is, she was sitting on a bench on the boat. The boat hit a wave. The boat went down. She went up. When she landed, she missed the bench and landed on the floor of the boat. She immediately lost the ability to feel or move from the waist down.

That was exciting.

She was airlifted to Boston and 48 hours later had surgery. We were told that she might never walk again and if she DID, it would be months before she'd likely even be able to put any weight on her legs.

Her surgery was on a Monday. On Wednesday (as in only 2 days after her accident), I was walking down the hallway in the hospital to see her and I saw her walking from her bed out to the hallway. Yep. Walking.

If you asked her then (or even now), "not walking was never an option". I know that sounds so ridiculous but it's true. She was going to do whatever it took to get the job done. And she did.

Now, let's not get too ahead of ourselves. She wasn't going to win any speed races right away. But she was walking. She got out of the hospital and went to rehab within a few days. Insurance wasn't going to let her go to the best rehab hospital in, arguably, the country. We told them otherwise (don't mess with us) and off she went. She started her first day of rehab the same day Maddie and Hannah started their first day of fifth grade. She was determined to learn more than they did that day. And, I'm pretty sure she did.

Within a week, she was home. We weren't all that comfortable with this timeline and thought that she should be under more constant care in rehab for a while but the doctors (and certainly she) had other opinions. They all said that she'd be fine. And she was. She hates, I'm sure, when we talk about this entire "event". But she's really a Rock Star. It needs to be talked about. A lot. It makes me believe that anything is possible. (Should I break into song now or later?)

She is impossible to describe in words. Not just from this whole stupid-ass "when she was going to be paralyzed" life event. But also from every other minute she is awake. (And that's a whole lotta minutes because the woman barely sleeps.)

My husband (her favorite son-in-law…you do the math) calls her "Ricochet Rabbit" and the "Energizer Bunny". She never. stops. moving. She starts one project, gets part-way done, starts another project, gets part-way done, starts another one, goes back to the first for a bit. You get the point. At any time of day/year, and this is no exaggeration, you could walk into my parents' kitchen and see her half-consumed cup of green tea, red wine, soggy cereal from the morning and leftovers from last night's meal all on the counter. (She will finish it all and then want more.) You could see the start of a delicious dinner being prepared on the stove, dry ingredients on the counter ready to go into the oven and homemade macaroni drying on the fireplace hearth. You could see the makings of a painting project, carpentry project (light carpentry, but still) and switching over decorations from one season to the next all while music is blaring in the background (usually "Sounds of the Season). You could see her gym sneakers on the floor as she just would have returned from the gym as well as her yoga mat on the floor of her bedroom from her pre-gym AM yoga session. You could see her grocery shopping list for my dad (because he is obsessed with Market Basket) alongside a list of Christmas gifts that she's already purchased for everyone in the family, alongside a menu for our upcoming weekend at the Cape, alongside FFF ("forced family fun") activities for said weekend.

Speaking of FFF, God forbid we all just "hang" when we get together. There must always be some sort of forced activity involving rules, teams, competition and winning (and if SHE'S not winning, we all lose.) She sweats while planning and executing FFF – even in the middle of the winter. She is crazed about FFF. Crazed, I tell you. Crazed.

My mom is on it. ON. IT. She rocks everything she does. If you ask her, she'd tell you otherwise, but she is an annoyingly incredible person - cook, entertainer, decorator, mom, wife, grandmother, friend, aunt, sister and cousin. The only thing she can't do well is remember directions, but she can't be good at everything…! She is thoughtful, kind, and determined as hell. She is funny, modest (I'd say to a fault), generous with her time and heart and – oh and did I mention she is determined as hell?

I think it's truly in my mom's family's DNA so I can't give her all the credit, but she is largely, I think, why I am a "glass half full" person. I mean she complains about stuff (just ask my dad…) and as her favorite son-in-law says, she often "yells" at people even though they've done nothing wrong and she's not even upset with them – it's just her way. But even still she has a good time no matter where she is, what she is doing, who she is with.

She is not even 5 feet tall, she weighs 95 pounds soaking wet and she eats and drinks like nobody's business. She eats all day long, will eat anything, will eat off of

26

people's plates (she usually knows them) and is not happy unless she's feeding someone a delicious bite(s) or alcoholic concoction. She appreciates if you don't drink, but she really doesn't support your decision. (I'm kidding, but it truly IS difficult to not eat or imbibe when she's around.)

She can tell people that they are driving her crazy, annoying and nuts but somehow, is not offensive. Not in the least bit. In fact, she makes you recognize just exactly why you are so annoying. And she makes you want to change your ways immediately.

Even though she doesn't feel comfortable meeting new people and making small talk (hmmmm...I feel as if I know someone else like that...), everyone loves her. And when I say "everyone", I mean "EVERYONE". If you don't love my mom, you are a complete loser. I don't mean to be rude to you (I may not even know you...) but it's true. A loser with a capital "L". (Please don't deny it. What's done is done.)

When Maddie and Hannah were little, my parents babysat them during the week. They never just "hung out" with my parents. They came home each day with arts and crafts projects, new exercise moves, homemade macaroni and a whole new wardrobe to show for their time together. All, courtesy of my mom.

Her Faith is unwavering. She loves her church, her beliefs and her religion. She believes. With her heart and soul.

I find myself, throughout the day, saying and doing things and I FREAK myself out because I am being my mom. In every way. (Well, as much as I am capable of. I wish I could be more like her, but I'm just not sure there's room for more than one of Her.) Hannah and Maddie often say/do/act like her too. I'm not sure they even see it yet. It hurts my heart when I think about how much of "her" is in "us".

My mom was sooooo young when she had me. I feel so blessed because when some women would have been selfish, bitter, self-centered and poor woe-is-me, she was always the exact and utter opposite of that. She gave me, gives me and will always give me 200% of herself. Always and forever.

As much as I can want - and try - to take credit for me (not that I'm perfect but I'm talking about the sorta okay parts), I can't take credit. It's all due to TMM, The Miracle Mom.
She honestly is The Best.

And she, truly, makes me strive to be a better person. Because no matter how much "better" I am, I'll never be as "better" as her. I mean, it's not a competition. I know that. She's not trying to be the best. She just IS The Best. In every way. I've learned to live with it. And I'm better because of it. And I can only hope that one day, I'll get there...

9 STEP PROGRAM

Step 1: Open up bathroom cabinet.

Step 2: Look inside bathroom cabinet.

Step 3: Put hand inside bathroom cabinet.

Step 4: Find full toilet paper roll inside bathroom cabinet.

Step 5: Take full toilet paper roll out of bathroom cabinet.

Step 6: Take empty toilet paper roll off of wall. (I know you noticed it was empty.)

Step 7: Replace empty toilet paper roll with full toilet paper roll (because it's already in your hand, remember?)

Step 8: Throw away empty toilet paper roll.

Step 9: Watch your mother do her Happy Dance.

Thank you for joining us today.

See you next week. (And please arrive early. We will be holding our monthly raffle.)

OL' TIMES

I spent the afternoon with a bunch of high school friends. We were celebrating the new journey into motherhood with our dear, dear friend. We are all so excited for her and can't wait to see her grow each day as a Mama. Isn't motherhood the best?

It was such a great afternoon. At the shower were a bunch of "townies" and spending time with people that I've known for decades+ makes me so happy. I love my hometown. I know parts of it are entirely dysfunctional but most parts of it make me very proud to be a townie too.

The high school friends that were there at the shower are awesome. First of all, they are all still totally (annoyingly) gorg and lovely. They are funny and they simply make me laugh. They are all amazing women, amazing wives and amazing mothers.

I especially love them because they "include" me. I don't mean to sound all junior high (although that would be appropriate because we all did roam the halls of Horace Mann together many moons ago). I say this because they were (and still are) "best friends". You know, they are an entire "come as a package" crew. They lived in the thick of things together, 24/7, for years.

I, on the other hand, am a layer (or two) removed from them. We've always been friends, but I wouldn't consider myself as a part of the package. I am happy to be included as an add-on to the package deal.

I know a lot of their stories. I have either heard the stories a few times over the years or I was actually there when it all unfolded years ago. (Sometimes I wish that I hadn't been there for some of their stories...) Now that I have daughters I sometimes re-think certain choices that I may or may not have mad. Don't we all, to some extent, feel that way about high school? Please tell me you feel this way too...???!!!

Anyway, I loved today.
I loved seeing how these women (myself included) have grown over the years. We all have done okay for ourselves. Better than okay, in fact. It's not always easy, being an adult, but we seem to be moving in the right direction. Let's hope this trend continues.

I loved being in my comfort zone. I don't like meeting new people (I hate this about myself, but it's true) so I always love when I can walk into a place and already know the who's, what's, and why's. Ya just sit down and pick up where you left off. It's so simple and easy. My husband thrives on meeting new people. Me? Not so much.

I loved seeing all their kids and by that I mean that I loved seeing only their daughters. There were no stinky boys allowed at the shower!! I am proud to be among such great moms. We all, for sure, have great role models. And we all are, for sure, thankful for this.

I loved talking about ol' times. I know, to some, it would seem as if we were stuck in the past. That's not it. It's just fun to laugh. It's fun to remember.

CRAZY TRAIN

This is one of my favorite pictures. I am about twenty-five yards away from finishing my second marathon.

Guy met me at Mile 25 and ran the rest of the way with me.

He drives me crazy, but I love him.

And as crazy as he is, he loves me right back.

FATHER TOM

This morning, I sang and played at a funeral for a man who worked at our church for many years. As I picked up the program and saw the priest who was celebrating the mass, it took my breath away. He was our Pastor for many years and, a number of years ago, he relocated to another parish so that he could be closer to his ailing mom. We exchange Christmas cards and his name is mentioned in our house a lot. He is a man that has had an impact on our lives like no other.

I have often said that we are very blessed to have a crazy number of people in our lives to whom we owe much gratitude and respect. They have helped to direct us, comfort us and shape us into the people we are today. We, along with our children, are remarkably blessed.

Well, this man is above and beyond anyone else in our lives in the way of a "special person." As Guy has said many, many times, "this guy is something special. You can't explain it. You can't understand it, but you definitely feel it."

During the time when we were lucky enough to have him serve as our Pastor, I talked to him about things that I've never talked to anyone else about. And I mean anyone. (My eternal thanks to Guy for suggesting that Fr. Tom and I chat.) The sadness and despair that I felt was unspeakable and we felt as if he were the only person that could see me through. Many, many tried and, for that, I am eternally grateful. But it was him and only him that said the words that I needed to hear. He knew just what I needed.

He is a "real" person who happens to "get God" too.

When I saw him this morning, he immediately asked about the girls and Guy. Oh, and he also told me that I look the same as I did on our wedding day. (Did I tell you that he was a very special person?!?!) Other than his clearly failing eyesight, he is great in every way.

Say what you will about the Catholic Church (and no offense taken, I've probably said it too…) but this guy, well, we are so blessed that he is in our lives.

SHE

She laughs.
She cooks.
She cleans, weeds, plants, creates, decorates, (did I mention she cooks <u>a lot</u>?) and entertains.
She knows this sucks.

She hosts people at the Cape house, all hours of the day and night.
She makes you eat and drink even when you really don't want to anymore.
She makes you eat and drink even when you really can't anymore.
She knows this sucks.

She walks to and kneels in church (for the first time in a while since the accident) because she finally can.
She smiles.
She knows how fortunate she is.
She also knows how much this sucks.

She plays with Hannah and Maddie and is the funniest person they know.
She cooks with Hannah and Maddie and is the best chef around.
She still only thinks of others.
She knows this sucks.

She won't let this get in her way.
Even though it does.
In every minute of every one of her days, it gets in the way.
It sucks. She knows this sucks.

She is truly amazing.

DADDIO

We spent much of this weekend with friends of ours who are having their second baby. They don't know if they are having a boy or a girl, but the dad is hoping that they have a boy. He doesn't think that he will understand how to have a girl.

It reminded me of Guy's reaction when he found out we were having twin girls. He went pale white and was speechless. The first words out of his mouth were "Oh my God, they are going to be thirteen one day..." He was worried about his overall cluelessness of being a dad in general. (He didn't have much experience with kids at all.) He was especially worried about his cluelessness of raising daughters. Two of them no less! At the same time!!

Well, suffice to say, he proved himself wrong in (literally) minutes. I'll never forget Day One in the hospital. He was changing diapers, wrapping them in blankets, talking to doctors, answering questions, asking questions, filling bottles and feeding two babies at once in no time.

Every day, since then, he has proven that he does, in fact, know what he's doing.

Every day, since then, he has proven that he was, in fact, <u>made</u> to be a dad to two girls.

He is a pretty balanced dad and, as a result, they are pretty balanced kids. They play the piano for him and they play football with him. Together, they watch the Oscars and the Patriots. They wrestle and then cuddle with him, all in the same breath. They laugh with him and ... well, they laugh at him. (Because, in addition to being wicked balanced, he's also wicked funny...)

C-5

There's a lot of talk about the Blizzard of '78 right now. Each year, around this time, people reminisce, but it is especially the case this week because we are expecting a pretty big storm in a few days.

This week, in 1978, my parents were the managers at Ledgewood Apartments and had been for years. In fact, they lived at Ledgewood before I was born until we moved to our house in 1977. Before, during, and after the Blizzard of '78, my parents had to spend countless hours dealing with "landlord-type stuff" at the apartments – plowing, shoveling, loss of power, etc. Only being six at the time, I needed someplace to stay because my parents were so busy.

Where did I stay?

Auntie Ellie's apartment. Apartment C-5.

My Auntie Ellie passed away a few years ago. She was 94. I had the unspeakable honor of delivering the eulogy at her funeral. (It still makes me cry when I think of it.) I am beyond words thankful to have had the opportunity to share with our family and friends my thoughts on this amazing lady. Among the thoughts I shared were some of my memories of Apartment C-5.

This place really was the hub of Ledgewood. It was where all of the repair and delivery folks, potential renters and current renters (not to mention their family and friends) and our family and friends knew they could go for a laugh, a drink, some food, a hug, a big juicy kiss –and typically ALL of the above multiple times over, simultaneously.

I spent a lot of time there and one of my most cherished childhood memories took place in Auntie Ellie's red recliner chair. I often wonder what happened to that chair. I would give anything to have it in my house right now. Auntie Ellie and I would spend hours in that chair. It was in the middle of her living room, overlooking the courtyard. She, in her snap-up-the-front apron. Me, with my pageboy haircut and cords. She'd say "Push over! I'm so fat! My big BEhind!" She'd laugh, I'd giggle and push over as much as I could so that we could both fit in the seat together. To me, the more squooshed we were, the better. We'd grab our songbook from the drawer and sing "Five Foot Two", "After the Ball", "Take Me Out to the Ballgame", "Side by Side", Ain't She Sweet?", "If You Knew Suzie" at the top of our lungs. We didn't care what we sounded like because we thought we sounded "just beautiful." It was pure joy for both of us. Pure. Simple. Joy.

Auntie Ellie gave me our songbook for Christmas in 1990. On the inside cover, she wrote, "Dear Kim. This was our special book. It has such beautiful memories. Love you. Merry Christmas. Love Auntie Ellie."

Our songbook sits in my jewelry box. I look at it a lot. As I read her handwriting, I can hear her voice and smell her perfume. I would give anything to be with her again. Just one more time.

Our songbook reminds me of her and of our time together. It reminds me of the love I felt in Apartment C-5. It reminds me that I want to be just like her when I grow up.

A-OK

I love when our children start a conversation with "I have something to ask you and it's okay if you say 'no.'"

Oh, okay. Thanks for your permission to parent and be a parent. Phew.

THE BABE

I recognize that attending a prom is pretty common. Most of us have done it. Most of our children will do it too. Now, as an adult, I recognize that it's really a night where your parents spend stupid money for a few hours of fun, but really you could have just as much fun ordering some pizza and playing music in the basement with your buddies and it'd be much cheaper. But I understand the importance to a teen.

I knew this day was coming. I'm not talking specifically about "the prom" itself. I'm more talking, I guess, about the fact that she's old enough, mature enough, no-longer-two-years-old enough to go to such an event.

Wasn't it just yesterday that she'd run down the hallway to my office, jump on my lap and chat with me with her pacifier in her mouth as I squeezed her bum? (Honestly, that bum was perfection.)

I can still see her re-enacting "The Nutcracker" in five minutes or less in the recital hall at FSPA. She never missed a single part.

Every time I hear "Jingle Bells" I giggle. Her one-of-a-kind performance of "Jingle Bells" on the recorder when she was six or so will go down in history. I can't do it justice here but the next time I see you, please ask me to demonstrate. I'll happily oblige.

How much time did we spend teaching her how to skip?
How many hours did we spend laughing at her as she tried to run in a straight line while she really was running in a circle, with one arm flailing back-and-forth, back-and-forth, back-and-forth much more than the other one?
How long before she realized that she could, in fact, speak while wearing lipstick and not get any lipstick on her teeth?

When did she stop calling me "Kimmy" and start calling me "Kim"?

It's not that I thought she wasn't going to go to her prom. It's not that I thought she'd forever be three years old. It's just that I can't quite believe that we are "here" already.

We, I say. I know it's not my prom. It's not even my kid!

But very rarely do you have the chance to see someone nearly every single day of her life, especially when she's not your kid.

Maddie and Hannah have many amazing people in their lives. People they look up to. People they love. How many times have they heard me say "Do you know how lucky you are to have so-and-so in your world??!!"

Well, this so-and-so has always and will always hold a special place in my heart. In our hearts. And as much as it likely brings her pain, to me, she will always be "The Babe."

SUMMAH

I try really hard, 365 days a year, to be a chill-and-take-life-one-day-at-a-time-go-with-the-flow-and-don't-let-things-ruffle-your-feathers kind of gal. Some days, my attempts are in vain. Other days, I get the job done.

It's amazing though how, especially at this time of year, it is so much easier for me (and probably many others) to just "be". We're not any less busy this time of year. In fact, we are probably, in many ways, busier. But there's something about July and August that make me not have a care in the world.

I THINK

I think – as much as I am having a great day, doing a little bit of this and a little bit of that, that my heart is heavy. Kev.

I think – he is smiling, watching Guy and the rest of his best buddies golf today at a tournament in his name, where they will laugh, drink good beer, reminisce, eat yummy food and just be together. His favorite things to do. Kev.

I think – they will raise money today for his children, not because his family needs it, but because they don't know what else to do. Kev.

I think – that as much fun as they are all having, they'd stop it all in a single breath to have him back. Even if for just one more minute. Kev.

I think – when I saw his mom and dad in the grocery store last week, it was all I could do to not start bawling in the produce aisle. When I hugged his dad, it was the closest I'd gotten to a "Kev King" hug in a few years. And I didn't want to let go. Kev.

I think – his wife is the strongest person I know. Kev.

I think – his parents and his brother have a hole in their hearts that is unspeakable. Kev.

I think – that I am so angry that his children will grow up without their dad. And every football that my husband throws to them in this lifetime will make me happy and sad at the same exact time. Kev.

I think – on my run today, my tears were the result of so many thoughts in my head, swirling around, that it hurt me to breathe. Kev.

I think – that my husband, one of the goofiest people I know, will never get over this. Ever. He will always be sad. Kev.

I think – these guys, who would do anything for each other and will always be there for each other, know that this is the biggest loss they will ever have. Kev.

I think – that every day, he is with them. Kev.

MULTI-TASKING

Dear Lady Driving By Me This Morning,

I appreciate the importance of dental hygiene, and kudos to you for not wanting to miss a day. However, please pay more attention to me and less attention to brushing your teeth while on the road and behind the wheel. Oh, and I think you missed a spot.

Yah, right there.

'MEMBA WHEN?

As I hang in my kitchen, making the kids' last lunches and snacks of the school year (YIPPEE!), I can't help but think back on my own school years.

Kindergarten: Knowing for the first time that I thought boys (well, a certain boy) was way cute. Tommy. Oh-em-gee, with the little bowl haircut. A-dor-able. I now teach his son and daughter and they are equally adorable as he was. Sometimes I see his expressions from when he was younger on their faces and it blows my mind. I also remember getting off the bus one day and Stephen kissed me on the top of my head as I walked down the stairs off the bus. I was mortified. Come to think of it – he was super cute too.

First Grade: Mrs. Wood reading us "Charlotte's Web". I've always loved that book.

Second Grade: Beautiful Mrs. Goss. She WAS Snow White. My mom always came in to the classroom to be a parent helper. I love that she did that. Amy and I both wanted Bobby to like us. I'm pretty sure he didn't notice either one of us. He'd totally like Amy over me now, for sure. She is so gorg.

Third Grade: Jessica had those super cool pencils with the troll/gnomes-things on the eraser end with the crazy hair. (You know the kind where you could twirl between your hands and the hair would get all zonky.) I loved being in the highest reading group. I used to be smart. I'm still not quite sure what happened...

Fourth Grade: Getting my first "F" in Mr. Gonsalves' class. I still don't quite understand longitude and latitude.

Fifth Grade: Charlie's messy desk. We'd come back from gym or art or something and our teacher, Mrs. Ficco, would have turned the desk over, emptying it all out, so that he'd have to organize/throw out stuff. He'd walk in, start laughing, and get to work. He never seemed annoyed. It was like he was just expecting it to happen.

Sixth Grade: Meeting Alyssa on the bus going to Central District. We ate devil dogs and nearly choked because they were so dry and we had nothing to drink. This was also the year that Guy teased me nearly every day in the cafeteria at lunch.

Seventh Grade: Mr. Ferrari and his rings. He was awesome. I wonder what he's up to these days.

Eighth Grade: Dancing with Bryan at a CYO dance. I was so worried that I looked like a hussy. We had, approximately, three feet between our bodies while we danced to some 80's love ballad, I'm sure.

Ninth to Twelfth Grade: Big hair, bright lipstick, pegged pants, the Franklin 500 and Danny.

Ah, those were the days.

AS KAREN CARPENTER ONCE SAID, "(THEY LONG TO BE) CLOSE TO YOU"

They can.
They certainly do.

And when they do, they are fine.
And perfectly content.

But if given the choice, they don't. They'd simply rather not.
No thank you.

If given the choice, they would much rather be together. As close together as possible.

We have told them since before they could understand our words, "You are stuck with each other for a minimum of eighteen years. You can make it wonderful. Or not. It's your choice. We're just here for the ride."

I think it's safe to say that they took these words very, very seriously.

When not in school, they are with each other. ALL DAY.
They eat, play, read, sleep, work and breathe together. 24/7.

And still, when they go to bed, they talk for minutes – sometimes hours – before they fall asleep.
And then again, in the morning, blah blah blah back and forth and forth and back.

Honestly, what in the HELL is there to still talk about?

It amazes me.
It always has.
It always will.

BFFs

The bald guy on the bike.
The lady with the hat.
The other lady with the dog, sometimes two.
The Italian Nonna.
The teacher.
The grandmother.
The holding-hands couple with the dog, sometimes two.
The running lady.

These are the people I see nearly every day when I run.

We wave.
We say "g'mornin'" and I wonder if they are closer to being done with their workout than I am (especially when it's three degrees colder than ridiculous.)

I make up stories about them that I think are true. In my mind they are entirely true. (But I HAVE been known to inadvertently start rumors.)
I worry about them when I don't see them.
I wonder what they do once they get home.

Is that weird?

Don't answer that.

I need a life...

MORE THAN FOUR

I sang and played the organ at a funeral this morning. There were only four people sitting in the pews. That doesn't include me, the priest, the lector, or funeral home attendants.

It made me sad.

It made me think of my funeral (…just for a minute and then I got creeped out.)

I wouldn't want guests to wear black.

Everyone would look great in orange. Or red. Brown would be okay too, I suppose.

The ladies should wear fabulous lipstick. And great funky rings.

The men should totally wear baseball hats. And I'd want Guy to wear a visor.

Sneakers, especially Converse, would totally be appropriate. In fact, they'd be encouraged.

I'd want little children to sing "The Rainbow Connection," "Sing," and "You Are My Sunshine."

I've been told that I know a ridiculous number of people. At my funeral, this would come in particularly handy. The more, the merrier. I'd want it to be like a big reunion. Lots of hugs and "nice to see you agains."

When it's over, I'd want a party. A big party.

With great food and drink (lots), 80's playlists (with a bit of 70's thrown in).

And laughter. Fall on the floor-tears streaming down your face-miss half the funny stuff because you're laughing so hard-laughter.

I'd want people to be assured that I was in a better place in Heaven.

Because I could see anyone and anything at any time from my viewpoint in Heaven.

Because I was spending my days eating and eating and eating and eating and enjoying every last delicious, heavenly bite.

Because I was living each eternal minute only with those that I love more than life itself. Every waking moment. While they walked the earth, I would be with them, really WITH them, with every single step. Whether they knew it or not. So, I wouldn't want them to be sad.

Because I sure wouldn't be.

I've lost some pretty amazing people in my life. And this is pretty much how I imagine them.

They watch over my family and me.

They keep us comforted and safe. All day. Every day.

Until they've had enough of our earthly shenanigans. Then they move on to the next crew who needs comfort and guidance. Then they do it all over.

Again and again and again.

On a regular basis, they all get together, have a great meal with wine and laugh about all the dumb things they see us do every day here on earth.

And believe me, we do a lot of dumb things…

HAPPY BIRTHDAY, GUYZEE!!

The first birthday I remember celebrating with you was your 21st. I remember thinking that you were "so old" and "so cool" as you went in to buy your first legal six-pack…um, I mean, your first six-pack ever…right, definitely your first six-pack ever…

I never imagined that all these years later, we'd still be celebrating. I guess I never really think about it but we've been together a long time. And it's been a relatively easy ride, I'd say, this Kim and Guy-a-Coaster.

You share your birthday with Big Bird, Bobby Orr, Carol Reiner and Mr. Rogers, to name a few. Not bad company, I'd say, right?

No matter what anybody else says about you, (I'm kidding, I'm a joker), you're not half bad. In fact, you're a real stand-up guy. (Except for when you're watching a Patriots game, because then you really leave a lot to be desired, quite frankly. I suppose, though, some people may find you entertaining in that situation. I just don't happen to be one of those people.)

You make me laugh like no one else. You laugh at me when I get angry with you. That bugs the shit out of me when it's happening but, after the fact, it's pretty darn funny. And you know not to laugh when I get REALLY angry with you.

You're the best Daddio in the land. And that's the greatest thing that you could ever, ever be. You work really hard at it. And you're doing a great job. Our kids are proof. They're not perfect. Neither are we. But I think they'll turn out at least half okay. Thank you for all you do for them.

Thank you for all you do for me.
You let me be me.
And I know that's not always easy.

But really, when all is said and done, this is how people picture you on your birthday. Because it's entirely accurate.

You're welcome.

THE SOUND OF SILENCE

On my 10+ miler today, this is what I thought about.

Yep. Nothing.
And that is one of the many reasons why I run.

BREAKIN' A LEG!

Tonight, the Franklin Performing Arts Company (FPAC) will hold open auditions for its upcoming production of "The Sound of Music."

Maddie and Hannah will be there to audition, of course. I remember, for their first audition, they were so nervous. They didn't know what to expect, what to wear, what not to wear, what to do, what not to do, what to say, what not to say, where to look, where not to look. And even though I could have filled them in (and then some) with what to expect, a) I sort of wanted them to experience it as everyone else did, and b) they wouldn't have believed that I knew what I was talking about anyway, so why bother!?!

Now, a few short years later, this whole auditioning process is second nature to them. And I love that. They are super excited and nervous for every single audition. That thrills me. The comfort level they feel with the process and the pride they feel for themselves – well, that thrills me even more. They're not necessarily going to set the world on fire with their abilities, but they love it. And truly, that's what's most important to us in our house.

It's not easy, auditioning. It's nerve wracking. You're throwing yourself out there for the world to see. And more often than not, you're not what the world is looking for. But the attitude and perspective that you go in with has the potential to help you grow so much. Not only as a performer, but as a person as well.

This morning, Guy and I had the same conversation with them as we've had many times already. It has become common language in our house. And yet, it is a language that we speak before every audition.

"Have fun!"

"Do your best!"

"You know how proud of you we are, right? No matter how proud we are of you – you should be even prouder of yourself."

"There are grown adults who would never have the confidence to do what you do. That's amazing."

"This entire process will help you – no matter what you end up doing in life!"

"You may not be cast the way you want to be cast. You may not be cast at all. Of course, you may be disappointed. That's normal. However, it is what it is. Things can't and won't always go your way."

"If one of you is thrilled about casting and the other one of you is not, we are equally proud of both of you. You may NOT gloat. You may NOT mope. You support each other. Always."

"Does this all make sense to you, these words that we have just spoken??!!"

They roll their eyes because they've heard it all before.
They roll their eyes because they know they will hear it again.

ALWAYS

As we head into the New Year, this is what I want.

To capture every one of these moments.

To keep this balance.
Of family.
Of work.
Of life.

To move faster, if I need to.
But remember that if I move too fast, I will miss this.
And remember that this is the speed that our family likes best.

To talk.
To listen.

To keep these three in the center of my world.
Always.

Oh, and to lose 15 pounds.
Always.

I'm just being honest.
Okay, 25.

360°

My life comes full circle a lot. I think it's safe to say that it does more so than a lot of others' lives. I guess living in my hometown ensures that I will bump into many folks who, for a number of reasons, bring me back. I like being reminded of my life when I was a child, a teen, a young adult. My life is what it is. I like to look back, think forward, learn from the past and apply it to the future. I am grateful for it all.

Today, my life came so full circle that it did a loop de loop right before my very eyes.

We had two Little Music School recitals this morning. Each was filled with family and friends of our youngest students, all enjoying a morning of music and lots of laughter. (Little kids'll do that to ya.) It was a great morning and it reminded me of why I love doing what I do.

In the recitals sat two women. They had different reasons for being there. One has recently re-joined our music faculty (to our sheer delight). She was there to support the program and see some of her students perform. The other was there to see her grandson perform in his first of (hopefully) many recitals. They both undoubtedly walked up the steps thinking that they were there to support the children in their lives under the age of five.

The funny thing is, the person they most supported this morning was another child over the age of forty. Me.

These women were my teachers when I was a student at FSPA decades ago.
These women are very much the "why" in why I do what I do.
These women, I'm sure, have no idea the impact they have had on my life.

In 1985, we were teenagers. Not unlike many FSPA students now. We were there because we loved what we learned there. We learned a lot, all the while alongside our best friends (and, by the way, we are still best friends). We were (we thought) way cool and, at the time, didn't look much past ourselves. We were consumed with our lives, our thoughts, our friends, our, our, our...we didn't need anything more at that time. (Oh, to be young again.) And to be fair, I shouldn't judge our younger selves. Isn't that what teenagers are supposed to do?

These women, though, knew otherwise. They, along with some other pretty amazing adults, always stopped, listened, hugged, held, supported and loved. Without question. Unconditionally.

This morning, as they were sitting in the recitals, listening to me speak about the LMS program (a program very near and dear to me), they both nodded their heads as they did so many times when I was a teen, working on a monologue or song. They nodded their heads and smiled at me, in support of me and what I hold near and dear.

Once again, decades later, they both stopped, listened, hugged, held, supported and loved me. And for that, I am eternally thankful.

ODDS ARE

"Rock, Paper, Scissors, Shoot!"

This is the ultimate decision maker/problem solver in our house.

Who will take a shower first.
Who will go to a make-up piano lesson, dentist appointment or haircut first.
Who will answer the door or pick up the house phone.
Who will choose the movie we will watch next.
Who will claim the dirty socks on the floor (even though "they aren't mine!!!")
Who will have the last bit of jimmies before we throw away the container.

It's funny but once the winner is proclaimed, there is truly no fuss, discussion or questioning.
It's a done deal.

Oh, how I wish all life decisions could be made so easily.

"COOKIE"

It was my uncle's birthday a few days ago. He is my mom's brother, one of the loves of my life, and I would do anything for him. The feeling is mutual, I know. Maddie called him because it was his birthday and, when he didn't pick up, she left a message. He called me later to tell me that her message cracked him up because it made him think of our Auntie Maffie. Auntie Maffie is always on my mind. I miss her every day. This is Auntie Maffie.

Auntie Maffie was one of my gram's two older sisters, the fourth of the six Pecci siblings. If you didn't know her, it is entirely impossible to get a clear depiction of her. Not a physical picture, not an emotional picture, not a social picture. Not any sort of accurate picture is possible. But I will do my best.

She had closets full of clothes, many things still with tags on them and yet she always shopped like there was no tomorrow. Pantsuits, skirts, full length fur coats, scarves, big jewelry, pointy shoes and boots, anything with sequins and bling – she owned it. Her husband, my Uncle Louie, would drive her to any store she wanted (she never got her license, which was probably safer for all others on the road) and sit in the car for HOURS while she shopped. I'm pretty sure he never complained or told her to hurry up. Not once.

She baked, really well, without recipes.

She loved her house down the Cape. She cried every Thanksgiving when she had to leave for the season. Her Cape house was her pride and joy. It connects me to her to this day. It always will.

She had trouble hearing and admittedly did not have much formal schooling. As a result of both of these things (in addition to the fact that she just didn't much care) she called many things by an incorrect (but close) name, no matter how many times we tried correcting her. For example, Wendy=Windy, Davis Thayer=David Thayer, Hannah and Madison=Hannison, Ocean State Job Lot=Ocean State Job Lock, Betsy=Bessie, Cold=Coal, Dupe=Pooxie, Spinal Ham=Spiral Ham. There are countless more. I kid you not.

She made THE most delicious salad (especially at the Cape). It was nothing fancy or all that special. But, man, was it good.

She would call every few days just to "keep in touch." She'd talk about the weather, what she had for lunch, and to remind us to wear a hat outside because it was getting "coal" out. (See word murders above.) And if you weren't there to pick up the phone, she'd end her message with "loooooooooooooove, Auntie Maffie."

She had no shame. None. If she needed to use the ladies' room and she was anywhere in the general vicinity (and by that, I mean anywhere in the house), she'd start pulling down her pants right then and there. I know that seems totally whack and it was, but man, was it funny.

She would walk by Uncle Louie, start humming or singing, and dance with him in the middle of the room. He'd never change his expression or even sing along. He just got up, wrapped her in his massive arms and danced with her. She loved to dance. In fact, I think that they met while dancing. (I'll have to investigate.)

Every birthday, she'd call and whether she talked to a live person or an answering machine (remember those?!), she'd sing the entire "Happy Birthday" song. And then, she'd sign off with "loooooooooooooove, Auntie Maffie". (As if there was ever any question as to who was on the other end.)

When Hannah and Maddie were little, for some reason, she called them both "Cookie". Then, they started calling her "Cookie". And the name stuck.

The fact that we all could so easily get on her Shit List was sort of a running joke in our family. If you didn't call, write, visit, visit enough, visit long enough...you get the picture, you heard about it!! It was just as easy to get off the list but we were all always on unsure ground!! It was sort of exhausting.

No matter what time of day, if you entered her house (and were at least, I'd say, 19), she'd offer you a shot of ginger brandy, Allen's ginger brandy. A "bukaruch", as she called it. (I have no idea how to spell it but the next time I see you, I'll pronounce it for you. You're welcome.) If you refused, she'd ask you a few more times and typically shame you into having one. If, somehow you had the courage and inner strength and held your ground and didn't drink it, she'd drink it by herself. It really didn't much matter. Now, whenever someone is coming to the cottage at the Cape for the first time, we all do a "bukaruch" in honor of Auntie Maffie. No one – and I mean no one – likes the taste of it. But we all do it. Because we have to.

When I was a teen, she would talk to me about boys. She would tell my friends and me to be sure to "keep our knees together." I mean, who SAYS that?!!?

If you were wearing something that she liked (and, although my description of her closet above does not demonstrate it, she had a great sense of fashion), she'd always say, "I like that. I gave it to you, right?" It was so funny. She always believed it to be true and most times we just went along with it. She, herself, always dressed impeccably, as she would say, "like a million bucks."

She crocheted and knitted like a champ. Auntie Maffie made some of this house's favorite blankets. I wrap myself up in them and it's almost like getting a hug from Auntie Maffie.

She loved the Red Sox and "Wheel of Fortune."

She always called Guy "The Surveyor." I'm sure she had no idea what he did for work but, to her, this was close enough. "How's the surveyor? He's lucky to have you. Does he take you out to dinner? He should take you out to dinner. Make sure he's not a cheapskate!"

As I said, Auntie Maffie never had her license and yet she would tell Uncle Louie how to drive. "Wait, wait, Louie. Now wait. Wait." I don't know what she thought he should wait for but he usually did because he was a smart man. A very smart man.

She always had a raging tan in the summer. And crazy long nails. And great jewelry. I wear one of her rings every day. Love.

Especially when she was getting older, she'd sit on her front porch at the Cape. In order to get to the beach, you had to walk by her. In order to not get on her Shit List, you had to stop and say hello.

She taught me to be proud of myself.
She taught me to stand up for myself.
She taught me to love myself.
She taught me to love my family.
She taught me to be a better person.

She was a one in a gatrillion lady.
And there will never be another one like her.

Love you, Auntie. Loooooooooooooove you!!!!!!!

WHO'S WHO?

Most days, I act (and feel) like June Cleaver.

But every now and again, a little bit of Mommy Dearest pokes through.

Our children are typically like the Ingalls sisters.
But even still, every night, I pray that they won't turn a corner and become disastrous human beings that you see in the headlines of the 6 o'clock news.

My husband is usually a cross between Ray Barone and Archie Bunker.

And now you know my Four Family.

TODAY

We spent the last week in NYC and DC. The girls and I visited the Big Apple with their BFF, Anna, and her mom, Kara. We had a blast, of course, and then the girls and I met up with Guy in DC. To say that this was a strange week to be away from home is an understatement.

We tried to keep up with what was happening in the news but it was difficult. I have to say that it was also nice, in a way, to be a bit removed from what was going on. We felt sort of guilty going on with our "normal" lives, but it was what made sense for us to do and I'm so glad that we did.

Two days before we left, the unthinkable happened on the streets of Boston during one of the most iconic marathons in the world. Our city's innocence was taken away. Our country's innocence was taken away as well (again).

Everywhere we looked, in both cities, there were flags flying, proud and strong and at half-mast. It nearly took my breath away at every glance I took.

It seemed as if, everywhere we looked, we saw folks wearing Boston Marathon jackets, Sox, Celtics, B's and Patriots jerseys and hats. More so than usual. It made me so sad and scared, but at the same time, comforted by the show of solidarity.

Hearing that NYC and DC were on heightened alert did make my heart skip a beat or two before we left home. It did make me question whether or not we should go at all. For more than a few minutes, I thought that it was a bad idea but ultimately, after lots of prayers, I decided that we cannot live in fear. We just can't.

They can't make us.

RECESSIONAL

Unlike yesterday's horrible funeral (is there really such a thing as a not-so-horrible funeral?), today I played and sang at the funeral for an 87-year-old woman.

Her only request was that a recording of her favorite polka was played as people exited the church.

Everyone left smiling and laughing.

Maybe it is possible to have a not-so-horrible funeral. That's the way to do it, folks.

MY NAME IS ZOOM AND I LIVE ON THE MOON...

Maddie and Hannah have, more than once, asked me what it was like growing up without a sister. (For many reasons, they can't imagine it.)

My answer is always the same. "Well, I sorta did."

I had a cousin and it is her birthday today.

Happy Birthday, Dee. I love you to the moon and back. All the way to Zoom's moon and back, in fact. I love you more than you'll ever know.

I can't even recount a fraction of our stories. It would take a lifetime.

It's probably a good thing that we don't live near each other because I'd not want to work or sleep. I'd just want to hang out with you and laugh. (We'd probably cry a bit too...)

I love everything about you. I always have (even when "life" or miles got in the way) and I always will.

So many times, in the middle of the day, I think of you and start to laugh. And I mean, like guffaw-out-loud laugh. I don't even try to explain it to anyone. It's our own little secret. That only we would understand.

Wahooie!!

I love you.

WICKED THANKFUL

You know those toy cars that, when they bump into a wall, flip around and do whatever they need to do to keep on moving forward? Well, that's my mom these days.

And on another note, as I was running this morning I was thinking about this year's Thanksgiving grace. Lots to be thankful for this year, folks. Lots to be thankful for.

IT TAKES A VILLAGE

Yesterday, a third grader, two fourth graders, two fifth graders and a seventh grader were facetiming their "big kid" FSPA friends who are spending their week performing and taking classes at Disney World.

The "big kids" were in EPCOT, saw a call coming from the "little kids" and took the time to pick up and chat. That's pretty ridiculous. And I will be sure to thank them when they get home.

A bit after the facetime, I got a phone call from a mom who is looking for a teen to babysit her two daughters this summer. I'm concerned that the mom thinks I'm making up how amazing this teen is. How could she possibly be as wonderful as I've made her out to be? (I really WOULD trust her to raise our children if we get run over by Mack trucks…)

Later this week, we will meet up with some other "big kids" who are very busy with their college-selves, but are taking the time to spend their day with us and our knuckleheaded children.

I am eternally thankful for all the "big kids" in our lives. However, it puts a lot of pressure on Guy and me to not mess things up. If Maddie and Hannah become total disasters, we have no one to blame but ourselves. They couldn't possibly have a better Village.

I AM S(N)O(W) ANNOYED

All I can think of is the beach.
And the sun.
And air conditioning.
And mosquitos. (Yes. I even miss mosquitos.)
And BBQ's.
And flip-flops
And sunblock.
And ice cream cones.
And a warm breeze coming through the window.
And dry streets that don't make running a near-death experience.
(No, I didn't run today. But I would like to someday soon. Will it ever stop effing snowing?!?!)

Ever??!!!

THE RACE

I had just finished my first marathon. I was about 25 yards from the finish and saw my family in the stands. I ran over to them, of course, and then ran over the finish line. I would have stayed chatting longer with them but my mom, (being the crazy closet competitive person that she is) could not believe that I was affecting my "time" by chatting with them!!

I didn't even see her in the stands, even though she was with my family. I wasn't looking for her because I had no idea she was coming. It was one of her (ridiculously rare) days off. Why would she possibly want to spend it there – a beautiful fall day, over an hour there and over an hour back?

After I crossed the finish line, I met up with my family. I saw her as I was hugging the girls. I couldn't believe she was there. She said she wouldn't have missed it. I honestly get teary every time I think of it. Sometimes, when I'm finishing up a run and I'm really done, I imagine seeing her on the side of the road, cheering me on. And I run a little bit faster.

If you had told me years ago that a) I'd have run a marathon and b) more crazily, that she'd be there to cheer me on, I'd have told you that you were on crack cocaine.

Friendships can sometimes be like a marathon. You just have to take it slow and steady. That first mile or two might be a little difficult, but once you get past it, the rest is a breeze.

LMF14

Valentine's Day was their anniversary. Uncle Louie and Auntie Maffie. Oh, Uncle Louie. I miss him so much.

As an adult, Uncle Louie was the first person that I loved with all my heart and soul that I lost. It absolutely slayed me from top to bottom. It slayed all of us. Losing him made me realize that my family was not going to be around forever. It scared me breathless.

Uncle Louie was a huge man. Broad shoulders. Massive hands. But when he smiled and laughed, he suddenly was the gentlest man I'd ever seen. He'd laugh so hard, his eyes would get completely squinty and his whole body would shake. He sort of laughed like either Bert or Ernie, I can't think of which one – but it made me laugh just to hear him laugh.

He introduced us to the Cape. Enough said.

Uncle Louie taught me how to swim. We could go out to the big Rock on our beach. He'd hold me and, even though I was scared, I knew he'd keep me safe. I'd hold on to his shoulders and he never let go. Until the one day he did. And I swam away.

Uncle Louie made THE best meat you'll ever taste. It was typically venison that he rubbed with some sort of salt and pepper mixture. (The bugger never told anyone exactly what the rub was, dammit!!) He'd put the venison on huge skewers and then cook them in a barrel in his backyard. As the skewer was done, he'd put the meat in a silver bowl on the table inside. Before he walked back out to the barrel to check the next skewer, all of us inside had devoured the entire bowl. His hands were so rough (he was a plumber) he could pull the piping hot meat right off of the skewer with his bare hands. I always found that amazing.

Uncle Louie played the organ. He's the first person that I can remember seeing play live music. I'm not sure that watching him play is what sparked my desire to play the piano, but I do know that I was amazed at watching his massive fingers dance over the keys. If I close my eyes, I can still see them as if it were yesterday.

His red and white polka-dot hat that he wore for quahogging still hangs in the house at the Cape. I can see him in the water, digging for quahogs. He'd bring them home and open them up for us, non-stop, at the sink in the backyard. He made it look so easy. We'd eat them raw with tabasco and a bit of vinegar. Still one of my fav summertime snacks to this day.

He taught me how to blow a bubble with gum. I remember sitting in the backseat of his truck as he drove and Auntie Maffie sat in the passenger seat. I was so afraid that I was going to spit out my gum at them. We were laughing so hard I thought we'd run ourselves off the road. He told me that we would not get out of the car until I learned how to blow a bubble. I did and then we did.

Every time there was an election (local or national), I'd go to Ma Glockner's with Uncle Louie and Auntie Maffie for dinner afterwards. It was our tradition. I think of this dinner every time I vote. He would order me a Shirley Temple every time. I never liked them, but I never told him so.

He was very proud of his country. If you helped him take down or put up the flag in the front yard, you'd better fold it or unfold it right properly or not help at all.

He had a teeny tiny radio on the mantle at the Cape that played swing music all the time. I think of him now whenever I hear the first note of that type of song.

Uncle Louie woke up at the crack of dawn. Always. When I slept over, and he thought it was time for me to get up, he'd take a broom handle and whack it on the ceiling of the living room which was directly below where I slept. Suddenly, we were up and starting the day, whether I wanted to or not!!

Because he woke up so early, Uncle Louie would typically fall asleep on the couch in the middle of the day, evening or nighttime like nobody's business. He'd snore so loudly that he'd wake himself up. I imitate him quite well and every now and again, Guy'll ask me to "snore like Uncle Louie" just to make us both giggle.

It occurred to me this morning while I was running that he always wore Converse sneakers when he went in the water. I think that the rocks and shells must have bothered his feet. (Too bad he didn't walk on his hands. Those things were strong as steel.) I wonder if he started my Converse obsession too?!?!

One time when I was in junior high, I stayed at the Cape without my parents and I apparently forgot to pack my belt. Uncle Louie went out to the shed and came back with a piece of thick rope that he thought I might want to use to hold up my pants all weekend. I was totally and completely horrified. I didn't want to hurt his feelings so I wore the goddamned rope all weekend!! When Guy and I got married many years later, Uncle Louie and Auntie Maffie bought us a great butcher block. Inside the drawer, he put a piece of rope.

In September 1997, I was sitting at the kitchen table when he told me that he'd just gotten back from the doctor's. He had cancer. He didn't know how bad it was. I wasn't concerned. This was Uncle Louie we were talking about here, folks. Are you kidding me? He was going to beat this. Easy peasy.

Guy and I got married a month later. He was already so sick by that point but he was determined to come to our wedding. Our photographer took a "Pecci Family Picture" and it is the last that I have of him.

He passed away two days before Christmas. I am so sad that he never got to meet Hannah and Maddie. He would have loved them. And they him.

TAKE ME OUT TO THE BALLGAME

There's just something about it.

No matter who wins or loses.

To watch a game (or even just hear a game in the background of your day) is magical.

It means that Spring is here (at least in this neck of the woods).

We made it.

Winter is over.

Thank you, Sweet Baby Jesus.

Go Sox!

H2O

11 weeks. 77 days. 1,848 hours. 110,880 seconds.

That's how long I was on bed rest while pregnant with Hannah and Maddie.

Everyone kept saying to me, "Enjoy this quiet time because once the babies are born, it'll never be quiet again." I understood what they were saying. I really did, but what I really wanted to do was get off my God forsaken couch!!

It was Sunday, November 10, 2002. My doctor had, two weeks earlier, given me the okay to start getting up and out a little bit. I was far enough along and the babes were doing so well. They felt comfortable with me being a bit more mobile. Some best friends ("forever friends") were in town and all meeting up at Holly's parents' house. I was thrilled to get out of the house.

We had a great night and Dupe was driving me home. (My stomach was too fat and my arms were too short. I could not drive. Keep your comments to yourselves, please and thank you.) As we were driving down our street, we were talking about the fact that I was worried that I'd not know when I was going into labor. She, who had already had one baby at that point, assured me that I'd know. My water would break and it would be painfully obvious. We did agree, however, that if anyone was going to be completely oblivious to the fact that she was actually in labor, it'd be me. Am I right or am I right?

Anyway, I hugged her as we literally finished our "you'll know when your water breaks" conversation ... and my water broke. All over the front seat of her dad's brand new car. And I should be sure to mention that it was a Lexus.

Dupe and I have had some impressive crack-up moments. None more so than right then.

I walked in to the house and immediately changed. Let's just say that there was no uncertainty that my water had just broken. Dupe went into the basement and announced to Guy and Sully that their game of darts would have to be put on hold as I was about to birth two children.

Guy and I left and, I assume, Dupe and Sully left right behind us. I honestly don't recall even saying goodbye. On the way to the hospital, we called my parents who were making homemade macaroni with Mary and Ray. (Obviously). We told them that there was no need to rush in to the hospital. It'd likely be hours before anything really exciting started happening. I'm pretty sure, though, that my dad was in the car before he hung up the phone.

I don't remember what Guy and I talked about on the way to Boston. I do remember being incredibly content. Our babies were finally here. I couldn't meet them soon enough.

BEST SISTER

They do nearly everything together. They are nearly inseparable. By circumstance as well as by choice. What one gets, the other one gets. Be it a shirt, a friend, a night out or a cold. That's the only life they know. They wouldn't want it (thankfully) any other way.

As I think these thoughts, there have a been a few times when this has not been the case. Maddie had a super cool, incredible, amazing opportunity to perform with Tony award winner, Beth Leavel, and Hannah was cast as Clara in the Franklin Performing Arts Company's production of "The Nutcracker".

Seeing one watch the other as she prepared and performed truly made my heart hurt. Were they jealous of the other? (Yes, they said so.) Were they bummed? (Sure, they said so.) But they were also good with it. (And, they said so.)

"It is what it is." (We told them.) "This is going to happen again." (We told them.) "You've got to figure out a way to make it work." (We told them.) "And so do we…" (We told them.)

And there is NO ONE in the audience or wings that is more excited for the Sister on stage than the other Sister. That's for damn sure.

They're good little eggs, these two. I guess we'll keep 'em.

LITTLE MAN

I think a lot about the people I miss the most. The people that helped me grow up. The people that aren't here as my daughters grow up.

I think about him.

His name was Ascenzio Bertoni but everybody called him Ausher. Well, everyone but me. I called him Usher Dupey. He was my mom's dad and I miss him every day.

I cannot listen to a Red Sox game on the radio without being brought back to the countless nights we'd sit on their front porch (me, my gram and Usher Dupey) listening to the game.

Difficult crossword puzzle? No problem. He'd solve it. National Enquirer? No problem. He'd read it.

"Patience" was not his middle name. It was surely a running joke (still is) in our family. He was small in stature, didn't say much, but you always knew EXACTLY what he was thinking. He'd roll his eyes, mutter under his breath (usually "Jesus Christ"), sigh heavily or just walk away.

He worked at Ficco's Bowladrome (what we called "the alleys" for years). When my dad first started dating my mom, they were both teenagers. As my dad tells the story, at one point, he said to my mom, "Your FATHER is the guy who works behind the counter at the ALLEYS?!!?" I'm sure my dad's voice had a bit of panic in it as he'd given my Usher Dupey plenty o' headaches over the years. Suffice to say, my dad was a bit of a "Dennis the Menace"-type. Regardless of a rocky beginning to their relationship, my dad and Usher Dupey ended up best buds.

When my parents built their house in 1977, my Usher Dupey wallpapered most of the rooms and hallways. (Ahhhhhh…remember the 70's??!!) I was only five but I remember him standing on a plank, balancing over our steps going upstairs, whistling "I'm Forever Blowing Bubbles." I was so impressed by his balancing act. In my young eyes, he may as well have been balancing over the Empire State Building. Come to think of it, I am known around many parts as a whistler. I wonder if I got the whistle bug from him…???

My dad and Usher Dupey walked me down the aisle at our wedding. No one knew, except the three of us, that this was the plan. He loved having our own little secret. As much as I love watching every single minute of our wedding video, seeing the look on his face as we walked toward the altar is one of my favorites. I tear up every time I think of it. I don't know who was proudest at that moment. Well, yes. Yes, I do.

He and my gram didn't have much but they didn't need or want much. When I was in eighth grade, my parents, my Auntie Maffie and Auntie Ellie (Gram's sisters) and my Usher Dupey visited family in Italy. While we were there, he bought a great looking pair of Italian shoes. I don't recall if they were super nice or expensive, but I'm pretty sure that he walked with an extra spring in his step every time he wore them.

He was proud of his church, St. Mary Church, in his hometown of Franklin. He donated years' worth of hours doing countless things – most notably serving on the Knights of Columbus, chairing the sausage, pepper and onion booth at the annual St. Rocco Festival and, of course, as an usher each Sunday at the 9 a.m. mass. He'd seat people if they needed seats (and would be annoyed if they arrived late) and he'd collect money from the collection basket. Every time he walked by me, he'd bonk me in the head with the basket. Every single time. Even when I was an adult. And I'd laugh. Every single time. Even as an adult. When he passed away, the ushers lined the steps of our church to honor him. That time, it was I who was the proudest.

For as many times as I told him that I loved him, for the first twenty-five years of my life he never said "I love you." To me or to anyone. Ever. Whenever we'd talk on the phone, I'd end with "I love you" and he'd say, "Yup, bye-bye" and we'd hang up. I don't know what changed for the last five years of his life but he just suddenly started saying "I love you too", out of the blue. I never asked why he started saying it. And I also never ever questioned his unconditional love for me. Ever.

He loved working in his shed. He'd cut out all sorts of wooden decorative things, cutting boards and such. He'd paint them and when he was no longer able to paint them, my mom would do it for him. When his hands weren't steady enough, he would color pictures and glue popsicle sticks around the edges to make a frame. I still have some of his creations and I will cherish them for as long as I live.

He was very good with numbers. I can still hear him spouting out figures, none of which seemed to make sense to me but that would result in the correct answer for whatever he was trying to calculate. I thought he was brilliant. Whenever I'm counting things, like chairs in a recital hall or people in a line, I think of him.

In his mind, if you weren't – at least – twenty minutes early, you were late. Plain and simple.

My Usher Dupey passed away on September 7, 2001 and his funeral was on September 10. The following day, of course, our lives changed forever as the horrible events of 9/11 unfolded. I am surely not comparing my Usher Dupey's passing to 9/11. However, just as everyone's lives changed on that week across the globe, so did mine. We said goodbye to my Champion. He was, for sure, my biggest love. I will never know love as I knew from and to him. I miss him every day. But I know that he is my Best Angel, as Maddie and Hannah refer to him. And for that, I have a little bit of peace.

WON'T YOU BE MY NEIGHBOR?

Yesterday, in class, it was brought to my attention that my eight- and nine-year-old's don't know who Mr. Rogers was.

I almost started to cry. Really.

I can't help but think about how much simpler life was when I was their age. (Pardon me, while I sound 95.) I'm not saying that he could solve all the problems of the world. I'm just saying that it was a start.

Do yourself a favor and look up some quotes from Fred Rogers. They'll make you want to be a better person.

Honestly.

SUN AND SAND

Going to the beach, for me, is definitely a roller coaster ride.

"Hmmm…I definitely look better than her and she's younger than me but CRAP – that lady JUST had a baby and she looks like that!?! Put down the chips, Kim!"

"If you kick me with sand one more time, I'm leaving you here and you can walk home. But, thankfully, you aren't complete brats like those kids. Sweet Baby Jesus, never mind, come kiss your Mumma. I love you."

"Oh man, I remember when my stomach looked like that. I'm so depressed. I need to go for a run now. But wait. Look at her friend. I look much better than her."

"I liked what I packed for lunch until I saw what that guy has over there. That looks so much better than my lunch. Damn. And I'm starving. But how did he keep that sandwich cold? It must have mayo in it. Oh, I like his cooler. I should buy a new cooler. Yep. Definitely need a new cooler."

"Why, oh why, did I not appreciate what I looked like when I was 23? Stupid! Stupid! Stupid! But wait, I wouldn't want to be 23 again for anything in the world. But then, I wouldn't have Hannah and Maddie in my life. That, I can't imagine. But if they weren't here with me now, there'd be nobody bugging me to open up the bag of chips without getting sand inside. Maybe I'll have just one chip."

"We really should leave. But I don't feel like packing up yet. Oh, let's stay a little bit longer. I hope we don't hit traffic. Please pass me the sunblock and get out of my sun."

I'm exhausted.

1-800-REALLY????!!!

So, a few days ago, we got a letter in the mail telling us that we were eligible for a "no strings attached" cruise for two to the Bahamas. Now, clearly, we knew that there <u>were</u> strings attached but I figured, "why not call when I have a few minutes and see what's what? Maybe we'd have to sit through a spiel about buying something, but if I can get a few days away in the sun 'for free' – sign me up!"

I had a minute today so I called and told the woman that I was calling just to get some information about the "deal." She filled me in and asked if I was ready to commit to the trip. "Oh no," I sort of chuckled, "I'm sorry if I was unclear. I really just wanted some information from you and, even if I was ready to commit, I would never do so without talking with my husband first."

She said (while annoyed), "Well, you are only allowed one phone call per mailing and your account was activated at the beginning of this phone call. You need to commit now or you'll never be eligible." "Oh, okay, well if that's the case, again I'm sorry (why was I apologizing?), but I'm definitely not committing to anything today. Thank you so much for your time." I'm probably biased but I really couldn't have been nicer.

The lady put me on hold and her manager came on the line. I went through my whole apology again (remind me, again, of what I did wrong??!!) and the manager went ballistic. And then hung up on me.

...so I guess we're not going to the Bahamas...

IT'S NO USE CRYING

So, I've pretty much gotten in trouble three times in my life. For reals. I know. I know. Weirdo.

It was 1978, Mrs. Wood's first grade class, Davis Thayer. I was wearing my favorite outfit. Navy blue corduroys (size 4T slim), a red and white checkered shirt with metal snaps for buttons that were really cold against my body, and a blue elastic belt with magnetic clasps that said "JEANS JEANS JEANS" in red. Don't forget the Dorothy Hamill haircut. I was rockin' the day and felt like a million bucks.

It was snack time at our desks. I don't remember who I was talking to but I apparently had a lot to say. (I usually did. Still do.) Mrs. Wood asked me many times to stop talking. I'm sure that she asked very nicely so as not to upset me (as I'm pretty sure I was her favorite...) but I just didn't stop talking. At one point, I decided that I'd had enough chit chat with my neighbor and I decided I wanted to talk to another friend. I took my whole milk carton (red and white, always slimy on the outside and always, always a bit too warm for my liking) and saltines (I haven't eaten them again since), went across the room and got the party started by the coatroom. As Mrs. Wood was about to turn around and catch me talking again (I'm sure she was starting to lose her patience with my cute little self) I ran back to my desk in hopes that she wouldn't see me. I didn't want her to have to talk to me again! That would mean I'd miss recess! Lose out on playing a round or two of 7Up? No way!

As I did, I knocked over my friend's milk and I got it all over my snazzy JEANS JEANS JEANS outfit! Nooooooooooo-oooooooo-oooooooooo!

The teeny tiny carton completely soaked my pants. (I was very tiny.) I had to go down to the nurse to get some hand-me-down clothes. A few minutes later, I returned to class in the same red and white checkered shirt with a pair of way too wide, long and bright purple, orange and green plaid bell-bottoms.

I was no longer rockin' the day.

Upon entering the room, I apparently had a bit of a 'tude toward Mrs. Wood. I was annoyed, embarrassed and a sight for sore eyes. She had taken my great fashionable self and, in a New York (Fashion Week) minute, turned me into a hobo!! I don't remember exactly what I said or did but whatever it was, it was clearly the last straw. I (and my five-year-old 'tude) had to stay in for recess. And I think I would have totally won 7Up that day too.

Dammit.

KEV

When I run, I have a lot of time to think.

When I run, I miss him. I picture his face in my mind with every step I take and I still can't believe that he is gone.

There truly are no words.

No words for the person he was. No words for how much he is missed. No words for how much he is missed by his best friends. All day. Every day. No words for the hole we have in our hearts. No words for how my husband was forever changed the day he so suddenly left. There are no words for the sadness we feel.

Forever, we will love you, Kev. Plain and simple.
Oh, and go Pats!

TO WHOM IT MAY CONCERN,

Dear Future Sons-in-Law:

I am trying to impress upon Maddie and Hannah the fact that simply hiding their dirty socks and underwear behind the trash in their bathroom does not equate with them getting washed, dried and/or ultimately put away. So far, I have not been very successful in my teachings. I continue, however, to remain committed to this process on your behalf.

Sincerely,
Your Future Mother-in-Law

*** and this one too ***

Dear Future Sons-in-Law:

This Future Mother-in-Law business is tough work. I feel as if it's only fair that I warn you. Currently, your future brides (yes, both of them) prefer to go to bed with "the day" still on their faces. Washing their faces with soap and water before bed seems to elude them. The fact that they don't seem to be bothered by their daily grime bothers me to no end. Equally disturbing is the fact that they insist that they simply forget to wash themselves. (We are clearly not dealing with rocket scientists here, folks.)

I had a complete FIT before bedtime last night (not my proudest moment) but when I closed the door, they were so upset they didn't chat with each other at all. They went right to sleep. They never go right to sleep. So, I guess what I'm trying to tell you is – whenever you want them to stop talking (because they like to talk a lot) just bring up the "sludge face incident" and they'll likely roll over and never say another word until morning.

On a good note, your favorite Father-in-Law went in to talk to them shortly afterwards (he is typically the "good cop") and told them it's not a big deal but that they should a) please start washing their stinkin' faces on their own time and b) please apologize for being knuckleheads and making me so annoyed and us so upset.

They apologized as soon as they woke up this morning. So, you'll be happy to know that they aren't too proud to say "I'm sorry". (At least we're doing something right…)

Oh, and while Guy is typically the "good cop", he will knock you into next week if you don't treat our girls well, so there's that.

Sincerely,
Your Future Mother-in-Law

GRAZIE

Thank you, little Italian lady, for giving me an apple and a peppermint candy as I ran by your house this morning. I do think, however, that you also gave me a bit of lint from your apron pocket as well. I could have done without that.

SHINE

Surround yourself with people that make you shine.
Life's too short to live any other way.

I WON'T GROW UP (I WON'T GROW UP)

I don't remember the details, but I was about Maddie and Hannah's age. My mom and dad had had some people over. Our house seemed to be "the place to be" most weekends (and probably most weeknights, for that matter) and my parents were cleaning up. At some point during the night, I woke up and got crazy sad. At the time, my dad was in the cellar vacuuming and I snuck downstairs and hid behind a chair.

When he was done, I snuck out from behind the chair, sobbing. (I can't believe I didn't give him a heart attack.) I remember being beyond words upset at the mere thought of growing up. I wanted things to stay just the way they were. I don't remember the exact conversation but I know my dad told me that, no matter how old we were, I'd always be his little girl. Talking to him made me feel so much better. I went back upstairs, fell asleep and never really thought about it again.

Until last night.

The girls got home from rehearsal and wanted me to lay in bed with them a little bit before they fell asleep. Quite frankly, I think they were a bit peeved that we didn't go to "the hang" after rehearsal. They, like their dad, don't like to miss very many social events.

We all climbed in to Hannah's bed, Hannah on my left, Maddie on my right. (If you're keeping track, the nighttime cuddle positions are opposite of the morning cuddle...but I digress.)

We chatted for a few minutes and Hannah fell asleep. Before I knew it, Maddie was asleep too. Suddenly I was beyond words sad again, but this time, I wasn't sad at the thought of me getting old. I quite like being older and wiser. (It's the grayer part that I can do without.) I just started thinking about how quickly these two girls are growing up.

Maddie and Hannah are rehearsing for "The Sound of Music." They are in the Children's Ensemble and, the folks who were cast in the Children's Ensemble last time our Company presented this show are now in college. We are still very close to many of them. They are fantastic adults, making great choices and living life well. But they are no longer cute little kids. They are adults. They buy me drinks at bars. Twelve years went by. Just like that.

I know every parent goes through it. I know we will come out on the other side just fine. I ask them these questions all the time. "Will you always hug me? Even when you're with your friends?" "Will you always laugh at my jokes like you do now? Even when you're super cool?" "Will you always love on me and be with me whenever I ask you. Even when you have other things to do with your friends?" They humor me and say "yes", but I will forever remind them of their answers in case they ever start to answer "no".

I'm just saying. I'm a little sad. I cried and cried all over Hannah's Taggie (given to her by one of those "I knew you as a kid but now you buy me drinks person and her family) as I cuddled with my babies.

When I snuck out of bed, they both woke up for a minute. Hannah said to me, "This is the comfiest I've ever been" and Maddie asked me "How'd you get to be such a good cuddler?"

"I learned from you both," I answered.
And then I cried a little more.

ETERNAL DOORS AND WINDOWS

Last night, Guy was finishing up some work in the kitchen and the girls and I were just sitting down to a few minutes of television before they headed off to bed.

Hannah proceeded to stand directly in front of me, completely blocking my view of the TV.

I said to her, "You know what Usher Dupey would say, right?"

Without hesitation, she said, "You make a better door than a window."
Without missing a beat, Hannah moved over so I could see, Maddie continued eating her snack before bed and Guy chuckled from the kitchen after hearing Hannah's response.

And I just took a breath and smiled.

He never met them. But they know him. And he surely knows them.

And for this, I am eternally grateful.

LIKE,

A few years into writing my blog, a very dear friend of mind told me that he had NO IDEA that I had a blog. I couldn't believe it. "How could that BE?" "What ELSE do people not know about me?" There are, I bet, LOTS of people who don't know LOTS of things about me (as if they care) like...

I am deathly afraid of not seeing my girls, their babies and their babies' babies grow up. It sometimes keeps me awake at night. As my head hits the pillow, I always end my prayers with "Please let me see my children, grandchildren and great-grandchildren laugh and play."

I will eat anything once. And chances are, I'll like it.

I am obsessed with watching documentaries and new stories about prison. And, probably because of this...

I sleep with a bat under our bed when Guy is out of town.

In college, I saw Winger perform at some seedy club in Providence and I somehow weaseled my way in the front row. I may or may not have grabbed Kip Winger's thigh while he was performing. I can't remember what he said to me but I know he said something...oh dear heavens, I'm so embarrassed now just thinking of it.

Guy is EXACTLY the type of husband I pictured I'd marry. My imaginary husband wasn't quite as much of a sports freak (I mean fan) as Guy, though.

Having a full (and huge) bowl of Fruity Pebbles makes me freakishly happy.

I regret that I still don't play the piano as much as I did in college.

One of my favorite, all-time movies is "Mommy Dearest." I'm not quite sure what that says about me.

I ran my first marathon in 4:12 and my second one in 4:05. Nearly every time I run I imagine what it would feel like to run "just one more" to see if I could shave off enough to run a sub-four-hour marathon.

The minute I finish a book, I can't tell you a thing about it. It's like I never read a single word.

I can no longer watch "Dirty Dancing", "The Outsiders" and especially not "Ghost" because I just can't believe that he's dead.

When I make Guy laugh, I am so proud of myself. 'Cuz I'm wicked funny.

I would pack our bags and live in Italy for a year if we, somehow, wouldn't have to worry about our mortgage. Guy and the girls think I'm nuts. But – YOLO.

If I didn't have my "real" job (which I love), I'd love to be an interior designer or a person who creates window displays. I'm not sure that I'd be good at either of those things but I think it'd be super fun.

I seem really nice and kind. And I am. But not always.

I'm starving. ... and we have Fruity Pebbles!!!!...

SILVER LINING

As I was sitting in the pick-up line at the girls' school today (in the pouring rain), it reminded me of our wedding day.

It was gorgeous the day before and beyond gorgeous the day after. It honestly hadn't rained on a Saturday in months. Until October 25, 1997. On that day, it poured and never stopped.

Leading up to our wedding day, we had obviously hoped it wouldn't rain. (Doesn't everyone?) But, the night before, when we knew that torrential rain was inevitable, my dad made a quick phone call. (Not to Mother Nature. She was busy getting ready to dump buckets on us.)

My dad called Mike, a kid we had known "forever", to see if he and his friends were busy the following day. The deal was, if they weren't busy, would they be willing to walk folks to and from the street, up the steps to the church underneath big golf umbrellas that my dad bought. They agreed to it and they showed up the next day, all dolled up. Too, too cute. I'm not even sure how old they were – 16, maybe?

I love seeing them in our wedding video. Still to this day, it makes me so happy that they ended up being a part of our wedding. They were the first people to greet guests. They chit-chatted it up with folks, laughed with folks and were just their generally lovely, adorable selves.

When I was standing in the back of the church, waiting to go down the aisle, they stood with us. In fact, one of them made sure that my train was straight before I walked down the aisle. I remember thinking at the time that if I ever had sons, I'd want them to be just like these guys.

We still see these "kids" from time to time. And I love to say that they did, in fact, turn out just the way I knew they would. Great husbands and dads. And they still make me smile.

I thought that the rain was going to be such a bummer. But it turns out, it is one of my favorite memories of the day.

You never know how things are going to turn out. Hopefully, you'll be very pleasantly surprised.

WHO KNEW?

They were little. Itty bitties.

One sister was taking a nap. The other sister was watching TV with Guy on the couch.

Suddenly, the sister on the couch said, "Daddy, Sister up". He didn't think much of it. The sister was still upstairs sleeping.

A few minutes later – "Daddy, Sister up".
No noises from upstairs. No nothing.

He walked over from the stairs and, sure enough, the sister came around the corner, awake from her nap, just as the other sister had announced a few minutes earlier.

Who knew? Sister did.

If you catch them just right in the middle of the night, you'll sometimes hear them talking in a language that no one has ever heard before. It is a language that only they can understand. One sister is clearly asking questions and the other one is clearly answering her. You can tell by the inflection of their voices. It only lasts for a few minutes but it's the coolest thing I've ever heard.

A few weeks ago, Hannah wasn't feeling well. It wasn't a big deal in the least. Toward the end of the day, she had rebounded and was outside playing, doing homework and having a grand ol' time. Guy and I thought that she was totally fine. At the end of the night, she fell asleep while watching TV. (That's not all that unusual as that kid falls asleep at an alarming speed, especially when she's relaxing with her Daddio.)

She hadn't even stirred yet and Maddie walked over to her with a look of total sadness and despair. Two minutes later, Hannah woke up, miserable all over again.

Who knew? Sister did.

Ever since they were little, one is brave and the other is hesitant. And then, for the next adventure, the roles become reversed. One is confident and the other one is afraid.

Who knew it'd be such a wild ride with these two?

Who knew? The Sisters did.
I'm not sure of much. But I'm pretty darned sure of that.

TAKE A BREAK

So, yesterday, the girls and I were leaving the library and my van wouldn't start. Long story short, I called AAA and when the repair guy came to tow me to our mechanic, the van started perfectly. (Isn't that always the way?) Even still, he wanted to check under the hood just to make sure that everything checked out okay.

He was unable to open the hood. I had the hood replaced a few months ago and have not needed to open it since. I told the AAA guy not to worry and that I'd just drive to our good friend who owns a garage. He could take a look at the hood and, in the meantime, see if he could figure out why I had trouble starting my car.

I pulled in to Robey's garage and while I was there, it suddenly occurred to me that, a few days earlier, my brakes had been making a weird noise. I mentioned it in a "I'm sure it's not a big deal but while I'm here I may as well tell you" sort of way.

Turns out, they were able to adjust my hood so that it opened without a problem. They weren't able to figure out why my car wouldn't start earlier in the day, but they didn't seem concerned so neither was I. Everything looked totally fine and they seemed to be completely puzzled.

They did, however, randomly learn that my brakes were nearly shot, with pieces falling to the ground as it sat in the garage and I, in no way, should have been driving.

Had my car started earlier in the day, my brakes would never have been looked at that day and who knows what would have happened.

Scary.

You may call it good luck. You may call it a lucky "break". (I'm here all night, folks.) I call it Divine Intervention.

It was my Gram's birthday yesterday. I think she gave me a present this year.

Thanks, Grams. I owe you one. Or two.

WHAT'S IN A NAME?

We spent such a long time figuring out what to name these babes of ours. And yet, we rarely call them by their given names, Hannah Faith and Madison Grace.

Instead, they are and forever shall be:
Boo-Boo
Bo-Bo
Lovie
Baby Girl
Sweet Baby Girl
Gorg Porg
Gorgie Porgie
Gorgie Porgie Puddin' and Piesie
Lover
Lover Bover
Love a Dove
Love a Dove Dove
Sister
Nu-Nu
Mi-Mi
The Girls
The Twins
The Ladies
The 'Naners
The Crazies
The Giggles
Thelma and Louise
The Rugrats
The Knuckleheads
The Goobers

When they were infants, I made up this song for them. (If you'd like to sing along, it's sung to the tune of "Clementine".)

"Mumma loves you. Mumma loves you. Mumma loves you. Yes, she does.
Daddy loves you. Daddy loves you. Yes, he does. [Kiss] Just because. [Kiss]
You're a coo-coo face. You're a crazy bean but we love you just the same.
And we always call you 'Sister' so you'll never know your name."
As my grandfather, Usher Dupey, would have said, "Call me anything. Just don't call me late for supper."

TIME FLIES

You know how some people draw hash marks on the doorframe to see how big their kids are getting? Well, instead, I use our guestroom bed as a guide. Each year, around this time, the bed becomes covered with Spring Concert costumes, dance shoes, tights and accessories.

Last night, after Maddie and Hannah went to bed, I organized their stuff. Each year, they have more stuff than the year before. And it was last night when it occurred to me that these kids, they are a-growin' up.

Last week, we watched old Spring Concert videos of them with tears running down our faces because we were laughing so hard at them. They were just little munchkins on stage – clueless and toothless – just doing their thing.

I love where they are in life right now. I try never to say "I wish we could go back to [fill in the blank]" because we can't. And really, each age (so far) has been a great age.

But I do have to admit that I miss "the olden days" with my babies.

HIT ME WITH YOUR BEST SHOT

I hesitate to write this because you simply can NOT get the gist of this part of my life. Unless you lived it. With me. If you are one of those people, you deserve a medal. You survived. If you are not, just do your best and read along.

I'm talking about my obsession with Danny. (And by "obsession", I mean the dictionary definition of "what a crazy person is.") I'm not sure if he is aware, now as an adult, of my obsession with him when we were younger. Suffice to say, that if he is not aware – but then reads this – he would rightfully be entirely entitled to relive his younger years and his Rock Star status, at least as far as I was concerned. And who wouldn't want to be a rock star?

I don't even know where to begin. I decided to participate in OSKEY my freshman year in high school. OSKEY was a high school variety show, for lack of a better word. At the time, it was the thing to do. Super fun tradition.

This particular year, 1987, OSKEY's opening number was "Summer Nights" from *Grease*. As a freshman, I was cast to sing the "Sandy" part and Danny, a senior, was cast to sing the "Danny" part.

Really, the story should end there.
"La, la, la…" You sing a song with a guy, take a bow…and move on. So, that's not what I did. I didn't move on. For a very, very long time. Moving on was impossible, in fact.

There's no need for me, here, to talk about his physical attributes that I found so appealing in every way – his hair, his clothes, his scar (yes, I said that), his earring. All you really need to know is that he was the lead singer/bass player in a rock band. Could he have BEEN any cooler?

OSKEY rehearsals started in February or so and the shows were in May, so for the last few months of my freshman year, I looked for him in every nook and cranny of Franklin High School. We clearly ran in different social circles so I rarely saw him – but man, I put in a good effort. As such, I barely ever spoke a word to him and when I did see him, I was lucky if I was able to string three and a half words together without drooling over my dorky freshman self. But still, every time we were in a shared (or even sort of shared space), it was obvious (to me) that it was clearly fate that brought us together. Simply a precursor to our wedding day.

He worked in the convenience store just below FSPA. How terribly convenient. He once sold me a Snickers bar. I saved the wrapper in a scrapbook.

He also worked at the gas station down the street. He pumped my aunt's gas once. And she saved the receipt that had his initials on it. Yep. That receipt was in the same scrapbook as the wrapper.

I related every. single. song on the radio to him. Lisa Lisa sang what was in my mind 24/7.

Any time I saw the color red, it sent me into complete and total alpha warp. I'm not really even sure why, to be honest. I have a faint memory of a red cloth hanging out of his pocket one day as he was working at the gas station. Maybe his car was red? His bass guitar? Interestingly enough, I don't recall now. But I certainly knew then.

When he graduated, I was a mess, as if he were leaving me. Now, mind you, we barely spoke a word to each other, but he was leaving me. Totally. I'm sure he was equally devastated. Totally.

I can't calculate how much gas money was spent driving by his house, every day, numerous times. I just HAD to drive by – multiple times a day – in case I caught a glimpse of him. That was always huge news.

When he left for college, my obsession did not end. In fact, it continued. In a very big way.

One night over his first Christmas break, as I waited in line to order (what I'm sure was a steak and cheese sub) at D'Angelos, I saw him just a few people in front of me. I did not go up to him to say hi. I was way too shy and he was a college dude now. No way, man. He ordered and left. I went home and sobbed on my BFF's shoulder for HOURS. Her shirt was completely (and literally soaked) with my tears. (Oh, to be a teenager again.) Come to find out (and I don't even remember how I figured this out), it was his brother in front of me - not him!! What a complete and total freak I was. As upset as I was at the thought of seeing him/not saying "hi", then not seeing him at all/he probably wasn't even home, I was more upset that I mistook his brother for him. I was clearly losing my obsessive touch!

For years, I wrote down every single time I saw him, saw a family member of his, heard a song that reminded me of him – you get the idea. It was totally annoying and obnoxious. Just ask my friends. To be honest, I can't believe they are still my friends.

There were many a song that made me think of him ("we" had many, many songs depicting our "relationship") but the one that most made me think of him was "Hit Me

With Your Best Shot." In fact, I STILL think of him when I hear this song.

For years, my ATM pin number = his home phone number. I kept that pin number for years until finally Guy (who had been my boyfriend at that point for years) was like, "Um, I really don't care (he and Danny were friends) but don't you think it's a little weird…"

My freshman year in college, I came home to give away my "Junior Miss" title. That sounds really dopey. Anyway, I was giving my little speech at the end of the show and, before I even finished my speech, who walked out to give me my flowers? Yep – in a tuxedo.

Are you effing kidding me?!?! I think I literally stopped my speech mid-word. My friends who were in the audience were cracking up hysterically in the front row of the audience. I don't know how I was able to stand.

We actually went out on a date shortly after that. He was a super nice guy, but he could hardly have compared to the rock star that I built him up to be in my head and I was, I'm sure, a complete dork so there's also that. (I'm pretty sure that he had a girlfriend when we went out on a date. I SO didn't care at the time, but I'm a bit horrified by that now.) Anyway, he kissed me goodnight and when the door closed behind me, I literally fell on the floor. Mature.

I still have my Danny scrapbook in my closet. Not because I'm still obsessed (I promise) but because when Hannah and/or Maddie come home, completely and utterly out-of-control obsessed with a boy (three years their senior who smokes and is in a rock band), I want to remind myself (and Guy) that all will be okay…

TICKET TO RIDE

Once upon a time, there was an ass.

His name was [fill in the blank with the current day celebrity who makes bad choices every day even though young children look up to him or her]. God help us.

The End.

I REMEMBER

My amazing cousins are spending their first night home with their delicious new baby tonight. It got me thinking about our Four Family's first night home as a family of four. Our Four Family.

I remember driving home with them from the hospital. I squooshed my big fat self into the back seat between the two of them because, somehow, I thought they were safer that way. I'm shocked that I'm not still stuck back there. I wasn't a small person at that moment in time.

I remember the big signs around the house that my parents made us. "Congrats and Welcome Home, Mumma and Daddy!" I wasn't sure who they were talking about. They couldn't have possibly been referring to us. (I was, in no way, ready to be a mother. In fact, I'm not entirely sure that I am even now!)

I remember talking to our neighbors (who are now best buddies of ours and our children) as they were standing in their yard when we drove by. They were going out for the night. I didn't think we'd ever go out. Ever again.

I remember a bunch of people coming over to our house that night. I couldn't fathom that there were two babies to add to the mix of this crazy wine-drinking, macaroni-eating crew. Not that I ever doubted it, but I knew that night, without a doubt, that this Village of ours was fierce and strong.

I remember my cousin, who was 2 ½ years old at the time, drawing all over our finished basement walls with a marker and not being fazed by it at all. I was amazed at that moment how quickly my priorities had changed. Literally overnight. (Oh, plus my mom got all the marker off before she and my dad went home.)

I remember trying to put them to sleep upstairs and one of them (I have no idea which one) had the hiccups. I couldn't believe that we were alone for the first time ever with these two and we were totally in charge. We. Had. No. Idea. What. We. Were. Doing. ("Please, baby, stop hiccupping. For the love of God, please stop!!")

I remember how we had to wake them up every two hours for quite a while during the day to feed them but, at night, when we would have appreciated a few extra winks, they woke up every two hours like clockwork.

I remember feeding them around 3 a.m. every night, thinking that I was the only human in the world awake. (Even the people on the other side of the world, where it was the middle of their day, were asleep if you asked me.)

I remember watching Guy wrap them up as "baby burritos", completely and utterly amazed at how natural he was with them, especially considering he'd not spent more than a few minutes with babies. Ever. In his life. Until he was responsible for growing two of them.

I remember Guy lifting up each baby burrito to his ear, pretending that it was a phone. "Hello?!!? Hello???!" He nearly gave my dad and Gram a heart attack every time he did it. It never got old.

I remember always putting Hannah's bottle on the left and Maddie's on the right. We had to be careful who belonged to what because we had to keep records of who drank how much for quite a while.

I remember twitching (figuratively, not literally) when one of them got dirty and the other didn't. I had to change them both because their outfits had to match – or at least coordinate. I lived in a constant pile of laundry.

I remember wondering if Hannah was really Hannah and Maddie was really Maddie. Oh God – what if we mixed them up!!

I remember not wanting either one of them to become dependent on anyone to fall asleep. Now, I'd fall asleep with them every night if I could.

I remember singing "Beautiful" to them. All day long. I still think they are both totally gorg.

I remember thinking that formula and bottles were the greatest invention ever.

I remember watching them sleep in the same bassinet and then the same crib, praying that they'd always want to be together. So far, all my prayers have been answered. BFF's.

I remember taking them to the store with Guy for the first time. It was pouring and we thought they'd melt. People literally followed us around the store. "So, did you KNOW you were having twins? How can you tell them apart? One looks JUST like you and other one looks JUST like him. Are they identical? Are you having MORE?!?!"

I remember taking them out by myself for the first time. It was so crazy cold that it literally took Hannah's breath away. I still imitate her on the first cold day of each year…I'm pretty sure she thinks I'm hysterical.

I remember. Like it was yesterday.

FRIEND

Do you ever wonder if there's anyone in your life that you've had a profound impact on and not even realized it?

I bet that happens to all of us. We are so busy going about our daily lives that we don't think about how we affect others. I think we also, sometimes, take for granted the relationships that we have with people and, as a result, don't recognize how special these relationships really are.

This morning, I thought a lot about a friend of mine. He is a friend to my husband. He is a friend to our daughters. He has, I am sure, no idea how much he means to us or what a big part he plays in our lives. Some days, they simply exchange a "hi" or "sure." Other days, they spend hours together. (Many times, more hours than he'd care to spend...)

But either way, he is a huge part of their lives. He makes them smile. He makes them laugh. He makes them think. He makes them wonder. He challenges them. He supports them. He is, beyond words, generous with his time, his effort and his heart. But if I told him, he'd not believe me.

That he doesn't see what a gift he is to all of us is truly a puzzle to me...
Our lives are so much more full (or is it so much fuller?) because of him...

So, thanks.

"...THESE ARE A FEW OF MY FAVORITE THINGS..."

Today, in class, I asked my students to tell us one of their favorite things that they did over December break.

I asked them to tell us only one favorite thing. If they told us more than one, we'd be there until next December break. But I'm going to list a whole bunch of my favorite things that I did over Christmas break. Because, well because I make up the rules at this party...'cuz you're all in my house...

- Walking around Boston with my Four Family.
- Watching Hannah and Maddie buy the "perfect" things with their Christmas present money.
- Sitting in our family room with some of my "forever" friends and those that loved us then and now.
- Watching old family movies with my cousins on Christmas.
- Sitting in my kitchen with friends, who are really family.
- Not wanting to have a birthday or a birthday party but then being so happy (as I am every year) when people show up. (HAPPY NEW YEAR!!!)
- Waking up at 6:00 a.m. and then going back to sleep until much later than 6:00 a.m.
- Singing the annual "Twelve Days of Christmas" on Christmas Eve.
- Watching and listening to my dad and Uncle Freddie play an old Italian game. (I have no idea how to spell it and will embarrass myself if I try.) I know these moments are limited and I cherish every one.
- All-day bedhead and pj-wearing daughters.
- Painting Hannah's dresser for her new room.
- Finding the perfect rug for Maddie's new room.
- Playing headbands with my cousins and laughing so hard I spit wine out of my mouth. Multiple times.
- Cooking. A lot.
- Knowing that, no matter what, the first thing Maddie and Hannah will do each morning is turn on the Christmas tree lights.
- Seeing the girls settle into their very own rooms for the first time ever.
- New Year's Eve traditions.
- Sitting at our office brunch laughing and laughing and laughing (and not always at my expense!!!).
- Asking the girls and their BFF if they wanted me to sit with them or without them at the movie theater and hearing a resounding "WITH!!"
- Knowing that we'll do this all over again next year.

FOR REAL?

I've heard this story a thousand times (give or take about 996) but I really should double check my facts before I share. Ah well...the following is *mostly* accurate.

Guy was in high school and had to complete an at-home health writing assignment. While having a serious lapse of judgement, he let a friend borrow his paper. Word on the street is that Guy understood that his friend was going to use his paper, simply, as a guide. I'm not sure where or how things got lost in translation, but apparently, his friend copied his paper word for word.

Guy was none too pleased obviously but there wasn't much that he could do about it at that point. They were in different classes and Guy hoped that, because they'd be turning in their papers hours apart, it would go unnoticed. (There is logic to that, I guess, when you are sixteen.)

A few days later, Guy turned his paper in during his class and had just settled in to his desk for the remainder of the lesson. No sooner did the class begin when the friend barreled through the door and says, "Sorry I was absent yesterday! Here's my paper!"

Yep - RIGHT on top of Guy's paper.

There was no way the teacher wouldn't realize that their papers were identical. They were both screwed. They sweat it out all night. (It may have been over a weekend so the stress lasted even longer, but I may be making that part up.)

They returned to school (on Monday...or whenever) pretty much anticipating that a trip to the Principal's office was inevitable.

Well, you'll never believe what happened.

The teacher's house burned down to the foundation the night before and everyone's paper was destroyed. Everyone in the class got an A.

ARE YOU KIDDING ME??

RED BIN, BLUE BIN

This morning, as I was dragging myself out of bed to run (it was just so nice and cozy in bed!!), I started thinking about when Maddie and Hannah were little. And how horribly sleep deprived I was. As tired as I was this morning, I was a gaBILLion times more tired, 24/7, when we had two babies in the house. Two babies – and one of those babies clearly thought that sleeping was an optional activity. And she all too frequently opted out! For two years.

Everyone always tells expecting parents "Get your sleep now while you can because once the baby is here, you won't sleep for years!!" Really, you hear those words coming out of the mouths of 1,408 people (give or take a few). However, you can't quite imagine it or understand it. Until you live it.

I have never said that having only one baby is easy. (I've never said that because it's not true.) But I have said that having two babies gives you permission to complain about being twice as tired twice as much. (I don't know if that's necessarily true, but that's my story and I'm sticking to it!)

I can see it so vividly. I was visiting work, having not returned officially yet. I was too tired to work. I was too tired to be awake. I sat in the hallway and cried. Sobbed. I. Was. Just. So. Tired. I knew how ridiculous it was and yet, at the same time, I wanted to jump off a cliff with no crying babies in the middle of the night in tow. I think my friends at work didn't know whether to laugh at me or cry with me. (Now, looking back, I hope they laughed at me.)

During the five days that we stayed in the hospital with the girls (and they were ready to go home in two – it was my body that had other plans), I remember the nurses telling us under no uncertain terms, "If you do nothing else, get these babies on the same sleeping and eating schedule." I can honestly say that I've never been given such brilliant and appreciated words of advice. If we were great at nothing else, we were great at keeping them on the same schedule. I am sure that some (and by that I mean all) in our lives mocked, joked, snickered, teased and called us names, because of our inability to go with the flow when they were little. We kept these two kids on a Gestapo-like sleeping and eating regime. And it worked. They ate, slept and breathed in sync. They sort of still do.

On Night Two of their lives, they were in separate bassinets in the hospital nursery and both girls were screaming. They wouldn't or couldn't settle down. The nurses fed, changed and held them. Nothing helped. Finally, they put Hannah in the same bassinet as Maddie. Immediately, they stopped crying and fell asleep. Needless to say, they slept in the same bassinet for as long as their little bodies would allow once we got home.

Because they were so itty bitty, we had to feed them every two hours for quite a while. Then, every three hours. Of course, wouldn't you know it, during the day, we had to wake them up to feed them. At night, they woke up for every feeding, right on schedule. They wailed. Even still, it all went quite well for a while, including the middle of the night feedings. Guy and I had a very good system going where we fed them together for some feedings and then we'd each grab a solo middle of the night feeding so that the other could sleep. We both got really good at feeding both girls at the same time. (In theory, that would help us get back to sleep sooner.)

We thought "we got this." Around four months, Maddie decided that sleeping through the night was a good idea and she never looked back. Bless her heart.

Then...well, then there was Hannah.

Sweet Mother of God. I can't even begin to tell you the torture that this kid put us through. The child could not, would not, sleep through the night. For two years. I know that it takes some kids longer than others. I get that. I really do. And obviously when she was an infant (as tired as we were) we knew that it came with the territory. But when she was older, the territory got old. And tired. People would tell us, "She's still only little. She just needs her mumma. She just needs to be comforted. She just needs a little pat on the back. She just needs a bottle." I'll tell you what she needed. She. just. needed. to. go. to. sleep.

Now, years later, with that miserable spot of life behind us, we tease her. I tell her about how I would say to her "choose the red bin or the blue bin. Which one do you want?" I was referring to the recycling bins. I threatened to put her in one of the bins in the middle of the night to fend for herself... (at least I was willing to let her choose which color bin!!) I just couldn't bear the thought of keeping her in the house some nights. She was the cause for nightmares...if ever she let us sleep.

Thankfully, during all of Hannah's sleep shenanigans, Maddie slept like a baby. Every night (and I do mean every night) we would worry that Hannah's screaming would keep Maddie up and then suddenly, we'd have two wailing babies on our hands. That never happened. I still find that amazing. Every now and again, you'd see Maddie raise her head from her crib mattress, cock her head to the left, look at her sister. "Dude, are you effing serious? Shut up and go to sleep! We get it. You want Mumma. You want Daddy. They'll be here in the morning. Unless you run them out of the house. Seriously, you're totally pissing me off. And you're REALLY pissing them off. Can't you see that??!." Then, she'd put her quiet little head down and go to sleep for the rest of the night. Thank you, sweet baby girl.

Meanwhile, Hannah was in her crib sweating, eyes bulging, face turning read, screaming. She wasn't hungry. She wasn't wet. She wasn't scared. She wasn't anything but awake. She was definitely awake. For hours.

We tried sleeping with her. We tried not sleeping with her. We tried rubbing her back. We tried not rubbing her back. We tried playing music. We tried not playing music. We tried feeding. We tried not feeding. We tried a dark room. We tried a light room. We tried an early bedtime. We tried a late bedtime. We tried a nap. We tried no nap.

And then, just like that, it ended. And the child who was once against sleep with every fiber of her being would, now, nap every day – perhaps twice – if given a chance. We're not done growing her, but so far, other than her few years of sleep madness, she's been one of the easiest kids on the planet. So, I guess you never know. You just gotta go with it. And see where it takes you.

NO THANK YOU

You know when you were little and you'd close your eyes when something was happening in front of you that you didn't want to see?

It took seconds, sometimes minutes, but when you closed your eyes, it was always gone.
As if it never happened.
The Bad Guy. The Monster Under the Bed. The Boogie Man.
If you just closed your eyes long enough, it eventually went away.

I've been closing my eyes for over a year now, pretending that something that was, in fact, happening, was not.
On behalf of a friend.

A friend whose family has been in my life for so long now, I can't even remember a time when I didn't know them. They aren't the "talk to them every day" friends. Or even the "talk to them once a month" friends. They are the "you know how much you mean to us, unconditionally" friends. You know, the kind that, no matter what happens, you know they are your "always be around for you" friends.

This family is fighting a massive fight quietly and with nothing but dignity.

They are amazingly strong. I honestly don't know how they are doing this.
They are in it together. From start to finish. Because that's how they do life.

I wouldn't be as strong as they are.
I am not as strong as they are.

Even I, from the outside looking in, cannot believe this is happening.
I am closing my eyes, from the very core of my being. From the deepest part of my soul. I am trying to will it away. But it's not leaving.

Dear God, it's not leaving.

Please, dear God, make it leave. Make it go away.

110

CROW

Enigma = noun; something that baffles and cannot be explained; something or someone that is mysterious, puzzling or difficult to figure out; secret, context, abstraction, tremor; a difficult problem.

That last one cracked me up.

If you know my dad, you can read the title of this chapter and understand where I'd like to go with it. And yet, you'd understand that I'm not quite sure where or how to start.

If you don't know my dad, you may just want to skip ahead because there is truly no way, and by that I mean NO WAY, I could explain to you my dad. Not on paper. Not in person. Not in hieroglyphics, braille or Morse code.

My dad, "Crow" to most everyone, is THE most loyal person I know. He will do anything for you, under any circumstance, if he is even remotely able, if you do well by him. If you do not, you can go shit in a hat (as my Gram would say). You WANT this guy in your corner. If he ever was, at any point, in your corner, and he no longer is, it sucks to be you. Your loss. 100%.

I can't remember a time when he didn't instill in me that it doesn't matter who you are, what you do, where you live, or how much you make – "you shit like everyone else". He treats everyone the same. And he expects to be treated as such. End of story. (Two shit references in one entry. That must mean something...)

He would honestly throw himself in front of a train for people he loves. Like, legit, no joke, across the commuter rail, at rush hour. The guy is serious business.

It's funny but I don't know much about my parents' relationship before they became my parents. Except that they've been together forever. I also know they became parents pretty early in life (generally speaking). And, as far as I can tell, this guy took his job as Dad and ran with it. He did enjoy his time raising hell and then some (and, if I may, still does) but when push comes to shove, this guy is all Dad.

And I say this not to be conceited. It's just true. I mean the guy loves me. I'm his only child. What more could I ask for? Um, what? Crow asks for grandchildren? Oh, okay, I'll step aside and let the royalty step on through.

So, I mean I KNOW that grandfathers love their grandchildren. I mean, that's their job, right? I'm not pretending that Hannah and Maddie's papa loves them any more than anyone else's papa, but...what I'm saying is that this guy is a legit papa. And, by that, I mean "legit, legit." Yes, that's a Crow-ism.

I've not covered the nitty gritty of how my dad actually got to be a papa, but it wasn't easy. It was quite a journey for all of us. I'm merely stating a fact. You have no idea. So, when my dad became a papa, he became a Papa with a capital P. There was NO ONE that was going to take that away from him. Because it almost didn't happen. But, fortunately, we live in a world where science can and does prevail.

And so, he takes his job very seriously.

When he ran an office supply business, he was The Man. It was his gig. For reals. I mean, he knows his stuff. (And I gotta say that I miss seeing him in action, in his true element.)

When he was the captain of a softball team, he was The Man too. (And I have memories of raging Sunday cookouts after their games for years on end.)

When he was the bartender, he served, carded, joked with, shit on, supported and loved every person who bellied up to the bar like it was his full-time job. Again...The Man

My dad can joke with the best of them. He can give someone shit and keep throwin' it, until they say "uncle". But my dad can also sleep in your nursery that's been empty for too long because he wants, more than anything else, for that nursery to be filled. (And he will never tell you that he was there while you were traveling in an attempt to pretend your life wasn't falling apart, but you just know he was there, 'cuz you know your dad.)

My dad pisses me off like no one else is capable of, and yet, he is also my net when I need to be caught. He is my blanket when I need a snuggle. He is my stop sign when I'm going into head-on traffic, and he is my hug when all other arms are tired.

He is my One and Only.

(NO) FUN IN THE SUN

We spent a lot of time at Horseneck Beach our junior and senior years in high school. It's funny considering how self-conscious we were – all the time, but particularly in bathing suits.

I remember one day in particular during our junior year, we were going to the beach with our "regular crew" along with two girls who were a year older than us.

I can't remember or imagine how long it took us to get ready that day.
I'm sure we each tried on no less than ten bathing suits each.
I'm sure we each used no less than ¾ of a can of Aqua Net on our bangs.
I'm sure we tanned extra-long in a tanning bed the day before a few days before so we'd be extra tanned.
I'm sure we didn't eat for days (well, maybe that was just me) in preparation.

Anyway, we got to the beach and set up camp for the day. We slowly took off our Champion gym shorts and laid down our scrunchy ponytailed heads on our towels. We knew we didn't look great. But we knew we weren't hideous. I mean, we were totally okay. And we were okay with that. Until we noticed what was happening around us.

It was as if the entire beach was suddenly and completely oblivious to everything else going on around them and could only pay attention to the beauty that was, let's call them "Jikki" and "Nulie", the older girls with us. Everything started moving in slow motion, quiet music started playing in the background, a slight breeze came across the ocean, and I'm pretty sure I saw Fabio riding a horse along the shoreline but he was far away so it was hard to make it out entirely.

They were perfection. Tanned, perfection, in white bikinis.

I'll never forget that moment of complete and total inferiority.

I'm sure we had a great time that day, although I don't really remember it. I think I must have blocked it out of my memory for fear of depression setting in.

Incidentally, "Jikki" and "Nulie" (okay, you got me - Nikki and Julie) are still gorgeous. To an annoying extent. But they are also still so lovely, it's hard to be annoyed.

Well, maybe I'm a little annoyed …and while I'm annoyed, please pass me the donuts. Nope. Not that one. I mean the Boston Crème. Yep – that one. Thanks. Delicious.

15 WEST CENTRAL STREET

This weekend, I saw what can happen when you don't let go of a dream. No matter what.

This weekend, I saw a community doing what was needed to git'er done. No matter what.

The weekend, I saw something really, really cool happen in my hometown.

There is now a real-life, living and breathing performing arts venue in downtown 02038.

THE BLACK BOX

Amazing.

BECAUSE HE CAN

We got an unbelievably horrible email today at work. A dear friend and former co-worker lost her husband unexpectedly yesterday. He was so young. 49. So full of life and smiles. So cute. That smile. That accent. We all walked around today, pretending that it was a normal day but knowing that, for his family, it was anything but normal. And even though we don't talk to them all the time anymore, we wish we could hug them and take away their pain.

Another husband gone too soon. Another daddy.

And so, as much as possible I will...

not be annoyed when he covers the entire bathroom counter with water each morning. Because he can.

not roll my eyes when he comes down wearing "that" shirt instead of the other one. Because he can.

let him navigate the road when I think we should be going another way. Because he can.

remember that, to him, a few extra minutes of sleep on the weekends means a lot. He will surely run his errands (and mine) later. Because he can.

know that, when Maddie and Hannah are being knuckleheads, I don't always have the right answers. He is doing and saying what he thinks is right to help them grow and learn too. Because he can.

watch him take five trips to the house with groceries when I would only take three. Because he can.

not lose my cool when he puts cookies directly on the table instead of on a napkin or paper towel. Because he can.

TRY to understand that, to him, if the Patriots win or lose, it really DOES affect his life. He adores every minute of watching the Pats play, win or lose. Because he can.

not be bugged when he hangs my pants on the wrong side of my closet (again) because at least he's doing laundry!! Because he can.

take the drain thing out of the sink and throw out the soggy cereal and not be annoyed that he didn't do it (again) because, really, it's not that big of a deal. Because he can.

The next time you say hello or good night or thank you to someone you love,
the next time you kiss or hug them,
the next time you are fortunate enough to spend time with them,
be sure to let them know how much they mean to you and how much you love them. Because you can.

CAN I HAVE AN AMEN, SISTER?

As a New Englander, my "I will run outside every day" New Year's Resolution would be much easier to keep if we celebrated New Year's in July.

Just an observation, really...do with it what you want.

TWIN PROJECT

When Hannah and Maddie were two years old, and then again when they were three, they participated in the Boston University Twin Project. In fact, they still get birthday cards from the folks at BU every year. I don't recall the details, but they were involved in a study that recorded their activity levels for 48 hours. Twice a year, they had to wear some sort of monitors on their wrists and ankles and then we had to go in to Boston where they were observed and filmed while playing and interacting with the interns at BU. It was a fun excuse to go out to dinner in Boston with the kids when they were done. (I wonder if this is what began their affinity for "big person restaurants" as young kids...)

Last night, we watched the videotapes of their sessions. First off, let me just say that it is hysterical to see them screaming and crying when I leave the room. The girls and I were cracking up watching them as they turned red in the face and flailed on the ground like complete lunatics. Guy totally cringed watching them behave like that (but secretly, I think he was a little bit annoyed that they were crying for ME and not HIM).

When they weren't screaming like lunatics, they were like mini-me versions of who they are now. So cool.

Hannah was soooo upset each time I left the room. Her face turned crimson and her little eyes totally bugged out of her head. She probably sweat through her clothes in nervousness and toddler-induced life stress. You could tell that she didn't like being unsure of what to expect next. She didn't miss a trick while the tests were being conducted and she watched every move that the BU students made. You could tell from the look on her face that she wanted to have a good time (I mean, how can a two-year-old not have fun with blocks, balls, movies, M & M's, goldfish and cars?!?) Eventually, she warmed up and had a blast, but I think for a while there the interns were thinking that they should have been getting paid for putting up with her craziness.

Now, years later, she is the same way.

Every. Single. Night. She asks us these same questions as she's going to bed.
"If we have a bad dream, can we wake you guys up?"
"Is the bathroom light on?"
"Are we going to see you in the morning?"
The answer is always "yes" but sometimes I like to answer "no" just to mess with her.

Every morning, at school drop off, she asks who will be picking them up and where, what we are having for dinner and if both Guy and I will be home at "the regular time." She is entirely fine if I give her an answer and then plans change during the day. She actually is a pretty flexible kid. She just apparently needs to know that there is a plan in place and she prefers to know of the plan, whenever possible.

She will be nervous each and every First Day of School Eve and she will rock the next day. Every single time.

During the Twin Study sessions, Maddie started out just fine. She walked in and owned the room. (Just like her daddy.) From the get-go, she played with everything and answered questions with a smile on her face. She talked to everyone (as much as she could at the time) and seemed to love this new adventure. Then, I think she must have heard my voice from the other room or something, and she (seemingly out of nowhere) lost her little toddler shit. She turned into a raving lunatic – a kicking, flailing, nutso kid. She rarely acted this way but watching her, you'd have thought it was a common occurrence. She was PISSED and there was no consoling her.

And she's still like this. She's pretty even keel and then BAM! She's crazed. She is totally fine and then something (which often appears to us to be the tiniest little thing) sets her off and she loses her mind. We look at her with our "are you serious?" faces, tease her as she walks away and then, in a flash, she's totally fine again.

She is not the least bit thrown off course by things that may throw most, but put her pencil in the wrong spot on her desk, fold her towel the wrong way or put her backpack in a different position and look out. There'll be hell to pay and she's taking names.

During this Twin Study, they had little bitty bodies and tons of hair, ponytails in all different directions, chubby cheeks and diapers bums. They had little voices and even little hands.

It makes me sad to see how much has changed … but then I think about what is yet to come … and I smile (and I drink some wine.)

THE INTERWEBS

Last night, this happened.

"Mumma, I have a question to ask you because you are a teacher. Well, you're not a real teacher. No offense, I just mean you're not a real teacher who teaches math or science or anything. You teach music. I mean you teach it really well and you're wicked funny when you talk to your students. And you're still smart anyway. Well, not as smart as daddy but you're still smart. Oh...never mind...I'll just google it."

Ok, thanks ... I was pretty busy anyway ...

WHEN ROSE COLORED GLASSES AREN'T ENOUGH

I think about them a lot. Especially when I run. More than most of you would imagine.

What would they look like now?
Would they be funny and do well in school?
What would their friends be like?
How about their favorite foods?
Would they be each other's best friends from the start?
What would they want to be when they grow up?
Would they love to cuddle with Guy and me the same way that their sisters do?
Would they love us to the moon and back?
Would he look like Hannah, as he does in my mind.
Would she look like Maddie? Because in my heart, she does.

If things had happened the way that (we thought at the time) they were supposed to happen, we'd not have been blessed with Hannah and Maddie. If we hadn't gone through all that heartache (and there's more heartache than most of you even know), we'd have had two kids and that would have been plenty. And perfect. And so, that means there'd have been no H and M.

And that thought obviously takes. my. breath. away.

And yet I still wonder.

Nearly every day.

BOOK 'IM, DANNO!

We don't have a football season in our house. We live football pretty much 24/7. I don't mind. It could be worse. It could be NASCAR. (My apologies to my southern cousins…)

Let's go back to 1997, for a moment, shall we? The year Guy and I got hitched. This will not be the story of how we got engaged. Nor will it recall how our wedding plans unfolded. It also won't retell how we delayed our honeymoon two days due to Monday Night Football. (Yes, you read that correctly.) This will be, instead, the story of how my husband got put in a paddy wagon and was PC'ed the night before our honeymoon at a New England Patriots' game. Yep. True.

Guy and I got married on a Saturday and left for our honeymoon on Monday night. Yes. We booked our wedding date and shortly thereafter, the Pats game schedule came out. We (and by that, I mean Guy) wanted to wait to leave on Monday (as opposed to the more typical Sunday) so that we could go to Monday Night Football. Of course, that was fine with me. (And not surprisingly, I won Wife-Of-The-Year after only being married for two days.) We decided to go to the game and then take a limo directly to the airport. We'd leave first thing in the morning for our much anticipated fun in the sun.

It was Pats vs. Jets. Or was it Green Bay? To me, it doesn't much matter. To Guy, it's surely an integral part of the re-telling. We, along with the typical tailgate crew, parked our cars at a parking lot within walking distance to the stadium and started walking over to the The Bus, where we would tailgate for a few hours before the game. We were about a mile away from The Bus. The Bus is where a whole bunch of Franklin-guys hang before/during/after each home Patriots game and eat, drink, play cards.

All was well. We were with best friends. It was a great fall night in New England. What could go wrong?

We needed to cross the street and a cop told us that we needed to walk a bit further before we crossed. OK. Fine. No backtalk. No attitudes. Just more walking. We eventually crossed the street and as we walked by the same cop again, he yelled something to us. I don't remember what he said exactly but it was completely and utterly uncalled for. To our crew's credit, they again let him do his thing and kept on walking. They had football on their minds. For a third time, a few yards further, our new BFF cop, appeared again and started giving us lip again. And again, (and I never give Guy so much credit) Guy and his buddies honestly didn't do anything to antagonize this cop. Even Kev talked to the cop in a way that only he could – gentle and kind – and nothing helped. Before I knew it, the cop was screaming at Guy, Guy was handcuffed

122

and thrown into the back of a paddy wagon. Happy Wedding Bliss, right?

We couldn't believe what was happening. We were close to the bus at that point and some of the bus guys came over to see what was going on. Some of them honestly thought that it was a practical joke. Nope. All real. It was so ridiculous and yet, a little perfect that it was happening to Guy. I can't really explain it, but if it had to happen to someone, it really made sense that it was him.

We had no idea where he was going or how long he would be there. (This was in the Olden Days before we had cell phones. Plus, how could he have used a cell phone? He was handcuffed to the floor...)

I enjoyed my time at the bus, had a few beers and asked if anyone could fit into Guy's bathing suit. We were all packed and I was going on the trip with or without him!!

Eventually, just as we were about to head in to the game, we saw Guy running down the street, away from the police station toward the bus. In my memory, I could hear the "Rocky" theme in the background but I'm pretty sure I imagined that. He had a booking number written on his hand but other than that, he was no worse for wear. Apparently, when they took him in, he told them what happened and they immediately realized that he'd (thankfully) not had anything to drink (yet) and that the whole thing was entirely stupid. Case closed.

The rest of the night was pretty uneventful. The Pats lost. We went on our honeymoon and had a great time. Needless to say, we re-told that story many, many times on our trip. And every time we told it, I was sure to say that I was going on our honeymoon with or without Guy. Hey – Drew Bledsoe was on the team at the time. We'd have had a great time in St. Lucia, right?

WHISTLE WHILE YOU WORK

We have an ongoing joke at FSPA that I whistle all day, every day. I mean, clearly, working in the environment that I do, I hear a LOT of melodies in the course of a day. How can I help it? They get stuck in my head. The only way to get them out is to whistle them out. (At least that logic works for me.)

I'm not even that good of a whistler. I'm really just marginally average. But that does not stop me. I'm all about the whistle.

I realized today, that I haven't whistled in over two weeks. To many folks, that wouldn't be that big of a deal. But to me, that's huge.

Well, today, I whistled again. I guess things are looking up in my world.

Baby steps. Literally.

AS CRUSH WOULD SAY...

It's not always easy. I always want to be able to.
But sometimes it's hard. Sometimes it's impossible.
Sometimes I just can NOT go with the flow.

I'm not sure how my cousins, Meg and Luke, would rate themselves on the Gowiththeflow Scale but as of last week, they became reigning champs and, if it's up to me, they will be for the unforeseeable future.

After months, heck, years of planning, a blizzard of EPIC proportions (like no one could be on the roads after 4 p.m. proportions due to a statewide driving ban) decided to rear its ugly wintery head on their wedding day. Long story short, the wedding was scheduled for a Saturday and it ended up being postponed until Sunday, the following day. In the end, it was a great weekend, fabulous wedding and incredible time from start to finish. All's well. But I'm sure that there were times when they wanted to jump off a cliff, a very high one, actually. They had to change their wedding plans so many times, make adjustments, readjust, change plans again and then again.

Who knows why their biggest day was messed with? But the general consensus with folks who attended the wedding is that we (as a general whole) tend to get so caught up in ourselves, we forget to look at the big picture. Maybe, because of the turn of events that weekend, other things happened that wouldn't have happened had the weekend gone off as planned. Conversations were had and moments were shared that wouldn't have played out exactly as they did had the Snowpocolypse not occurred.

We'll never know what could have been or what was, but it really makes me think.

Instead of overthinking every. single. moment of why, just go with the flow.

Why not?

SNOOZE BUTTON

You know when you wake up from a nightmare and you are so relieved that it's only a dream?

Well, this ain't that, folks

If you believe in the power of prayer and positive thought (hell, if you believe in witchcraft and Ouija boards), we could really use it 'round these parts.

PICKY EATERS

It is really important to me that we have a "real" meal as many nights a week as possible. Sometimes that means we don't sit down until 9:15 at night but, to us, it's worth it. I have a big binder of recipes and I try to pull new recipes from it as much as possible. I love that I have standard dinners that my Four Family loves, but I try to break out of the routine every now and again.

Over the weekend, I plan what I will make each night for dinner and make sure I have all that I need before my head hits the pillow on Sunday night. It takes more planning than I care to exhibit some weeks but, in the end, I'm always happy that I did it.

It all sounds great. Family dinner. Homemade meal. Fresh ingredients. Yes, yes, and yes. But in the process, I've created monsters. Food monsters.

Earlier this week, I realized that I was short a meal and I didn't have time to run to the store. I remembered that we had some frozen fried chicken and tater tots in our basement freezer. (I like to have stuff like that on hand if we ever have some little peeps over who may not like what's on the menu.)

Most children would have been thrilled. Fried yumminess with catsup and ranch dressing. Yum. (I did throw a cucumber on the table to make it at least remotely healthy...) Well, apparently these two are not like most children.

At bed that night, "Mumma, what happened tonight? You didn't even bread the chicken yourself?!? Those tater tots weren't even seasoned, huh?!? Are we going to have another meal like this? Ever?"

Really? REALLY???!!

Don't get me wrong. I love that Maddie and Hannah love food. But really?

REALLY?!?!? Monsters.

INSERT { HAPPY DANCE} HERE

Today turned out to be the day that my mom knew it would be. My dad has his doubts. (And I have to admit, I had my doubts too.)

MY MOM'S BACK BRACE IS OFF!! THE BRACE IS OFF! THE BRACE IS OFF!

My dad and mom were talking to her surgeon today. During the conversation about the accident, her surgery, her recovery and rehab, he (again) called her "a miracle." I'm sorry but that will never get old to me.

Now we just need to sit back and watch my mom work her magic. But I think there's something much, much more than magic at work here...

GIRLS WILL BE...DADDY'S GIRLS

We knew we were having twins early on in our pregnancy.

That was a blessing beyond measure. It took us a while to wrap our heads around that little tidbit of info.

About five months in, we found out that we were having twin girls. Literally, the first thing out of Guy's mouth (poor thing, he turned pale as can be and was speechless for a few seconds) was "Oh my God! They will be thirteen someday...!!!"

He couldn't imagine having one girl, let alone two!! His family is quite small. No sisters. No girl cousins. Guy is a guy's guy. All pat-on-the-ass-swear-in-your-face-watch-football-drink-beer-eat-cheetos kinda guy. Two girls??!! What in the hell would he do with THAT?!?!

Well, suffice to say, he has well figured out what to do with that. They are Daddy's girls, through and through. I just sit back, watch and smile.

Today, as I came home from running errands, the three of them were in the front yard, covered with winter hats and gloves, playing football, yelling plays and talkin' smack.

I'd say he's doing just fine.

LEGACY

I was asked to sing at a funeral this weekend.

I was honored to have been asked. While I don't know the family very well, our families, it seems, have always known each other on many levels – through church, friends, school. They are a family that I have always held in high esteem and I always will.

The funeral was filled with folks that, to me, are the foundation of this town. They are the families that have been here for generations and, likely will be, for generations to come. While everyone was so saddened by this sudden loss, there was a lot of comfort in seeing so many amazing people gather together to show their respect, love and support for this man and his family.

I am humbled to have had even a little, itty bitty part of the day.

The brother of the gentleman who passed away spoke at his eulogy. Four of his five children spoke as well. All of them spoke with an eloquence that cannot be described. As I sat and listened to these amazing words, I was in awe hearing of the legacy this man has left. Simply by doing nothing other than "being himself." He was an awesome (in the truest sense of the word) man. Husband, father, brother, uncle and friend. I sat in the church and was overcome with sadness for the people in his life who will miss him so much.

It made me wonder what my legacy will be. Now, I know (or at least I hope) that I still have years to go before someone's reading my eulogy… and I guess I don't need to panic just yet. But really. If I were to die tomorrow, what would my legacy be?

I'm pretty much just a Converse and jean wearing forty-something-year-old who gets through the day by making fun of herself, her children, her husband and, pretty much, anyone else in her way. That won't make for much of a eulogy. My legacy is weak, at best, at this point.

I guess I need to start working on building my legacy. But I guess you're not supposed to know that you're doing it. It's just supposed to happen.

I guess I'll just have to wait and see how it all pans out. Tick, tock. Tick tock.

SOMETIMES...

...I wonder if I could accurately explain how happy I'd be if my "southern" cousins and "northern" cousins lived closer to me.

...I envy how Guy can "work" a room at a party.

...I think about what (or who) I look like beside a "Kim". Pam? Lisa? Kelly?

...I laugh when I'm singing in church and realize that I don't need a microphone. Having a loud voice is in my DNA.

...I am amazed, thrilled, and terrified at the thought of raising two daughters.

...the laundry can wait.

...the dishes in the sink, however, cannot.

...I practice tap steps in my kitchen when no one is looking. I can still do a mean double open time step.

...I eat my lunch before 11a.m. and then I'm depressed for the rest of the day because it's all gone.

...it's easy to be nice.

...it's not.

...I am in awe at the speed at which I can change into comfy clothes after work.

...I can eat an entire sleeve of Oreos without anyone noticing that I even opened my mouth.

...I am off the charts embarrassed at how little I know about so many things.

...when I pull into this driveway, I wonder why I'd ever want to be anywhere else.

...I think about my best friends who are scattered around the country and I laugh at them. Man, they are funny.

...I think we should get a dog. (And then I realize that's ridiculous.)

...I take out stuff to dust and then remember that our cleaning lady will be here soon so I stop. (Is that bad?)

...lose sleep at night, worrying that I won't live to see my grandchildren and great-grandchildren.

...I just sit and listen to Maddie and Hannah laugh. And then I smile.

...I feel like I could run forever.

...I say "I could spit nickels" and then I am sad because it makes me miss my Gram.

...(usually) I am so full and yet I eat more.

...I am amazed that I've not lost these sunglasses.

...I wish I could just lose these damn 15 pounds, dammit!!

...dinner just has to be ice cream sundaes.

THE RIDE

I remember very vividly the first time I rode my bike down Union Street, on my own, without my parents. I remember being so excited as I "raced" down (what seemed at the time) the monstrously dangerous hill. I remember feeling very grown up and free.

This weekend, down the Cape, we spent a lot of time on our bikes. I was nearly always the "caboose", with Guy, Maddie and Hannah taking turns in the front. I was able to spend a whole lot of time just watching the rest of my Four Family together from this vantage point. I couldn't hear what they were talking about, but I could tell that there was a lot of goofing around, laughing and smiling between the girls and their Daddio.

You can't script these moments. And they are the ones that I cherish most. I try to notice as many of them as I can. I know that we will always have these types of moments but I also know that, soon enough, I will blink and these two will be riding on their own too. Literally and figuratively.

I'm not sure I'm ready for it.

A LADY AND HER PRINCE

Not too long ago, a dear friend and his wife (to us, they are family) heard that word that no one ever wants to hear.

Cancer.

The prognosis was not good. Stage Four.
("I'm sorry, but say that again. This can't be right. There must be some sort of misunderstanding.")

I remember exactly where I was when I found out.
I remember where I was when I talked to them the next day.
I remember not wanting to call. They needed some time.
I remember wanting to call. I wanted to hear their voices.
I remember needing to call. I needed to hear their voices.
I remember when we told Hannah and Maddie. Oh God, that was one of the worst moments of my life.

The thing is, though, there is simply no way he wasn't (and as I share this) isn't going to go down without a fight. I say this meaning no disrespect to people who have lost their battle. They fought the fight too. They were strong. They wanted to beat the odds. Why didn't they?

Who can ever even begin to understand why some people suffer and others don't?
Who can ever even begin to understand why horrible things happen to some and not to others?
Who can ever even begin to understand why amazing people suffer terrible things?
Who can ever even begin to understand why some people win this battle and others don't?

We will never understand. But I do understand this.

If ever in a situation like this, I will never give up. I will never let the people around me give up.
Because I've seen things that I never thought possible become possible.

The good guy doesn't always win. Life sometimes sucks. But, at least in the end, if you don't give up, you can say with all your heart that you gave it your all.

This man, whom I love with all my heart, doesn't know the meaning of "give up."

And this lady, whom I love with all my heart, will never give up right by his side until forever.

She is a Lady and her Prince. And we love them both with every breath we take.

They have taught me so many things.
And they have taught me this.

THANKSGIVING

I am thankful for...

Hannah's and Maddie's morning cuddles.
checking off another day of no diet coke.
seeing everyone so busy at work but always (well almost always) laughing.
beautiful flowers on the trees on my way home from work.
avocado and tomato salad.
seeing some "forever friends" who have known me since I was a kid.
not having any laundry to do.
texting besties back and forth all day as if we were with each other just yesterday.
homemade sauce for dinner.
having friends that I can call and ask "Hey, can you take the kids for a few hours?"
having friends that can call me and ask "Hey, can you take the kids for a few hours?"
knowing that one of my best friends is blissfully, unquestionably, breathlessly, madly in love.
catching up with a friend, even if only for just a minute.
sending Guy a link for the gift I want for Mother's Day. Thank you, in advance.
a freshly cut lawn.
watching Maddie and Hannah navigate a computer.
our Four Family walk around the neighborhood after dinner.

It's never a perfect day but if you pay attention, there are lots of near perfect things.

OH, NO YOU DON'T!!!

You learn something about yourself every day. Sometimes when you least expect it.

This morning, I was about eight miles into my ten+ mile run. A woman rounded the corner on Pond Street on the opposite side of the street. She was minding her own business and is a lovely person, I am sure. She was not paying the least bit of attention to me.

Unbeknownst to her, we were suddenly in a race.

I am probably the least competitive person you'll ever meet.
Until I suddenly feel compelled to be competitive and then, look out.

I ran so fast for the last few miles that I pulled a muscle.

But I won. BAM!

Now I'm home icing my leg. bam.

NYE

I try to run every New Year's Eve, regardless of weather or schedule, so that I can start the New Year on a good foot.

It occurred to me today that Guy and I have spent over twenty-five New Year's Eves together. That's a whole lotta auld lang synes!

Although he INSISTS that the thought of us being together MUST have occurred to me before this, he "professed his undying love" for me at Michael Dorsey's NYE party in 1990. (Well, he professed it as much as a twenty-year-old kid in a New Kids on the Block t-shirt could.) Truthfully, although we had been friends for years (we even double-dated a few times but not with each other) the thought of an "us" had never occurred to me. But the minute he spoke a few words (oh, and the kiss helped too), it became painfully clear to me that I had missed something that had been in front of me the whole time.

We got engaged on New Year's Eve, six year later. We were with our best friends and I was completely surprised. To this day, it still bothers him. "Dammit! You mean I still had a little more time left?!!?" (As if six years wasn't long enough??!!)

Going in the Way Back Machine, my parents were on their way to a NYE party in 1971 when I decided that it would be a good time for me to make my unexpected entrance into this world. Three months early. That was exciting. They clearly didn't have a chance for champagne or a visit with Mr. Clark that year. Because I was very premature and quite unhealthy, they didn't even win a toaster or fridge for my being one of the first babies born in 1972. I was in the hospital for months but eventually came home and well, all's well that ends well, right?

For all of these reasons, NYE has always meant a lot to me.

No matter where you are, what you do, who you're with – be safe tonight.
Be with folks that you care about and that care about you.
Be happy and kind.
Be the best person you can be. Tonight and always.

Here's to a New Year.

RIDICULOUS

I'd have been really angry if someone had told me that I couldn't marry Guy because he is a guy and I am a girl.

That'd be completely asinine, right?

I find it incredible that, in this day and age, there are people that truly believe that a guy shouldn't marry a guy and a girl shouldn't marry a girl.

Sometimes I am embarrassed to share the same planet with these idiots.

Love is.

Period.

BIG FAT CRABBY PANTS

First of all, that says "crabby" not "crappy." That would be an entirely different situation. One that I hope to never be a part of.

Big Fat Crabby Pants. That is what we call Hannah and Maddie when they are a bit off of their "A" game and in need of a smile and a chill out session.

Actually, more appropriately, it should be spelled bigfatcrabbypants. It is to be spoken fast and unapologetically. I have no problem telling them when they need an attitude adjustment.

It is what it is. And isn't that my job? If I need to deal with them when they are in a mood with a 'tude, they are going to know about it. (Those who have seen me interact with my children know that I rarely hold anything back. I tell them like it is. All the time.) Some may say too often.

Well, yesterday, it was not the children in the house that were the bigfatcrabbypants. It was most definitely the mother. For absolutely no reason, I couldn't wait for the day to be over. (And to be honest, the father was a semi-bigfatcrabbypants but he, at least, had good reason. His beloved Patriots did not have the best outcome on the field one day earlier. His crabbiness tends to linger when this happens. It's not pretty.)

There were a few select moments when I was not crabby yesterday but they didn't last very long. I quickly went back to bfcb, very very quickly, and seemingly without warning to those around me.

Here was my day. I slept in. (Who doesn't love more sleep?) I watched the inauguration on TV. (We live in an amazing country.) The girls were lovely and well behaved and played with their buddy all day long. (Our girls and their buds are rock stars). I left for work. (I love my job.) Guy painted our bedroom walls and ceiling that were in desperate need of a new coat of paint. (It looks great. He didn't get any paint on the bedspread or carpet.) He hooked up the printer. (We've needed one desperately.) My classes are well prepared for their show next week. (See above.) I came home and we ate a yummy dinner. (There's not much that can make me happier than a good meal.) I had no laundry or homework to deal with. I went to bed.

I know. I know. There is nothing in that day that warranted me to be even the least bit crabby. And yet, I couldn't get the crabbiness out of my way yesterday. I was miserable. I couldn't stand being with myself. I couldn't stand not being with myself.

So, today, I knew I had to remedy the situation. After my run, while getting ready for work, I immediately put on mismatched socks, one from Maddie and one from Hannah. I wore my high-top Converse. I packed a big bottle of (no, not wine...) tabasco in my bag to go with my homemade soup for lunch at work.

And the day went okay. Now I'm home making another yummy dinner. Yesterday is just a distant memory. I think I've turned the Crabby Corner. Thank goodness. For small crabby miracles.

THURSDAY NIGHT

The Cosby Show
Family Ties
Cheers
Friends
Seinfeld
ER
Chinese food take-out

These things have been our tradition for years on Thursday nights.
Now we have a new one. And it's our favorite tradition of all.

Spending dinner with a dear friend and his two lovely daughters. Every
Thursday.
I cook.
Kids play.
We laugh.
We cry.

And it's all good.

Very, very good.

IT'S A BIRD! IT'S A PLANE! IT'S A...IT'S A...

This morning, while getting something out of a dark corner of my closet, I came across two capes. I mean Wonder Woman and Superman-type capes. Real deal capes. Sparkly and fabulous. One with a big "K" and the other with a big "G". They were made for us in 2001 by dear friends of ours, Holly and Alex. They had learned that we had just fought (and WON) a huge battle with our (at the time) insurance company. This is not about that battle. You must read about <u>that</u> story with a full glass of wine in hand.

Anyhow, I came across the capes just before my run and it made me think about being a superhero.

I wouldn't want the ability to fly. I don't really love flying, to be honest, and I get lost driving to Milford. I'd be a disaster in the air. Especially with wings.

I'd love the ability to eat whatever I want. Now that would be super. But that's not the super power that I'd most like.

If I could choose, I'd love to have the super power of Fast-Forwarding. I'd like to be able to fast-forward through the shitty parts of the day, the week or life and get to the good stuff. I'm feeling as if this super power is a bit passive aggressive but, hey, it's my super power. It can be whatever I want it to be.

For instance, I'd love to fast-forward from the end of my shower to already having my hair dry. I hate being cold and wet. Under any circumstance. Well, except when I run in the rain. I love that.

I'd love to fast-forward past small talk at parties. If I never had to talk small again, I'd be a happy camper.

I'd love to fast-forward from turning off my computer at work to wearing my pjs at home.

I'd love to fast-forward from my freezing cold car in February to my nice toasty backyard in July.

I wish I could fast-forward and have my feet in the sand immediately upon arrival at the beach. Any beach. Anywhere. Any time.

It'd be great to fast-forward from walking into a car dealership to driving off with a new car. All that banter is so awkward.

Being able to fast-forward over Best Make-Up and Best Sound Effects and get right to Best Movie would be great. Of course, others would disagree.

On New Year's Eve, I'd love to fast-forward to the part when a super cute couple gets engaged. I hate all the bands anyway. I am old.

Right now, I'd love to fast-forward to when the laundry is folded and put away, the dishes are clean, tomorrow's lunches are made and the trash is put outside for early morning pick-up.

Sounds like I don't need a super power. I need a maid.

SHARSIES

"Home Alone"
That was the movie.

"Peaches"
That was the restaurant.

Me: "Are you going to finish your fries?" (as I reached over, grabbed the rest of the fries off his plate, finishing his dinner and mine.)

Make no mistake and despite what he may tell you, he clearly knew what he was getting into from Date Number One.

JUST CALL ME "NORM"

Today, I took a "Townie" run. By that, I mean, with seemingly every step, I was reminded why I, quite simply, love my hometown. I came across people, places and things that totally brought me back to my youth. Big time.

I ran by the house where my great-grandparents raised their six children, Uncle Tilly, Uncle Tony, Auntie Ellie, Auntie Maffie, my Gram, and Uncle Freddie. I only knew four of the six but they were and continue to be amazing influences on my life. Now a two-family home, my Uncle Freddie still lives in the upstairs apartment with his wife, my Auntie Jan. My two cousins, Uncle Tony's granddaughter, live in the downstairs apartment. That house, to me, is where it all began.

I ran through Fletcher Field. It is where I spent time swinging on swings with boys who broke my heart, with boys whose hearts I broke, and with the boy who won my heart.

I ran by a number of people who called out "Crow!" or "Hey, Crowley!" as I passed. I've known someone for a long time if that's what they call me. And, as always, it makes me smile.

I ran past The Rome. A local hot spot for generations, our kids have grown up knowing if you want a good pizza, make sure you go on a Friday when Rocco is in the kitchen.

I ran alongside two softball fields. One of them is where I met one of my dearest and oldest friends. And at the other one, if I close my eyes, I can still see my cousin Took playing softball with my dad, Johnny Tav, Mr. Gruseck, Johnny, and Dana, to name a few. I can picture my dad crouching behind home plate wearing his green and yellow 00 jersey.

I ran through the "new" high school. I am so excited that the girls will attend this state of the art facility. And yet, I am sad that they won't walk the halls of B Wing or stand in the concession line where Guy and I did at FHS. They will have arguments with their best friends, student/teacher conferences, infatuations, dances, shop class, report cards with fabulous A's and not-so-fabulous F's in a building that I don't know.

I moved over on the sidewalk to let Mr. Pisini pass by me. He was on his way back to his shoe store from the bank, where he (and I know this sounds odd) gets his daily cup of coffee. He has posters in his windows made with marker and poster board. If you look closely, you can see the marks he made with ruler and pencil on the poster board so that he was sure to write in a straight line. When you drop off shoes for him to repair, he gives them back to you in a brown paper bag like a tuna sub. He charges you, tops, $5.

I ran by a home that recently caught on fire. I saw the F & P Molla construction sign in the front yard, giving a shout-out to a tried and true Franklin company that (once again) is helping out those in need. (Why hire anyone else?)

I ran by a few of my oldest friends' parents' houses. It is so comforting to me to know that, inside, are people who know me through and through. And these same people would drop everything if ever I needed anything. With just a simple knock on their door.

I know that to some, maybe even to you, the idea of living this type of hometown life is cringe-worthy. I get that. I honestly do. But to me, I can't imagine living any other way. I completely understand why some people live far, far away from their hometown and hometown peeps. I am envious of those that have the chutzpah to leave all that they've known and start over – whether they be ten, thirty or fifty. There is absolutely a part of me that would love to pack my family and me up and just start over. Somewhere new. Somewhere different. But then, I think, "Why?" I really and truly do love it here.

The purpose of my run this morning was not to re-live my younger years. The intention was not to feel like the Mayor of Franklin. (I leave that honorary distinction to my husband.) But I am glad that I did.

MOVING ON

Today, I didn't get a run in because we are in the middle of our second weekend of "The Little Mermaid". It was a gorgeous day, weather-wise, and it's supposed to snow on Monday, so I'm especially bugged that I didn't get out.

Anyway, as I was working the box office at THE BLACK BOX, a woman that I didn't even recognize, came up to me and was going on and on and on (and on) about how amazing Hannah was in "The Nutcracker" as Clara. It caught me so off guard. That production was three months ago but it feels as if it was three decades ago.

It was such a big deal as we were living it and we, of course, were – and still are – beyond words proud of her. But, just as we told Maddie when we were dealing with the whole "your twin sister is Clara and you are not"-thing, once the curtain goes down after the last performance of a production, people move on to the next one. I love that. It doesn't allow for folks who "got the part" to make a super big deal about it, and it also doesn't allow for folks who "didn't get the part", to dwell on it. There may be a next time. Or maybe not…

There is so much to learn in this world where we find ourselves raising our kids. Yes, they learn how to shuffle off to Buffalo, sing in three-part harmony and differentiate between upstage, downstage and center, but they really are learning so much more.

More than I could ever explain here.

ONE STEP AT A TIME

The girls were little, maybe one and a half.
They had recently taken over the entire house and were into EVERYTHING!
Not coincidentally, this is about the time when Guy and I started to go a bit gray.

I was in the kitchen. They were in the playroom.
I heard the hustle and bustle of two nearly two-year-olds.
And then I heard silence.

I walked into the playroom, not knowing what I'd find.

What I found was Maddie, all askew, diaper bum in the air, head stuck between two bannisters on our staircase going upstairs.
Hannah was just staring at her, I think, clearly knowing that something was wrong but not quite able to articulate what exactly was wrong. ("...I mean, things had been going so well only moments before, Mumma...we were having so much fun with your cool pots and pans...")

So, I ran downstairs to the cellar, returned to the bannister and sawed the child out of the bannister.

And this one of the many times, early on, when I realized that parenting really only works with a ready stash of wine on hand. Always. It WAS almost noon...

TWELVE BAGS

Twelve bags.

That's it.

It's what (at the least) we've promised ourselves that our Four Family will donate to the Franklin Food Pantry this year. We can – and I'm sure we will – give more. At least one bag each month.

We want Hannah and Maddie to understand that when we are all out of double chocolate chocolate chip granola bars it is not all that tragic.

If we have to use raspberry and lime shampoo because we are all out of misty rain, we will survive. (And Guy will smell nice and fruity to boot!!)

When there is not more ziti downstairs and we have to have medium shells for dinner instead, life will go on.

We want to remember that there are people, right here in Franklin, that have trouble making ends meet. People they may go to school with. People that they see every day.

We want them to know that we can help.

We want them to know that they have helped.

I am so thankful that Guy had this idea. It's so easy to do it. So now we are.

THE TABLE

Yesterday, I was sitting in my kitchen, waiting for some lady to get here to do my physical so that I could renew my life insurance policy. Ho hum.

Anyway, it reminded me of the time when Guy and I were getting our first dining room table delivered. It was one of our first "real" purchases together (other than our actual house) and I was so excited. We both had to work and couldn't be home for the delivery so we asked my grandfather, Usher Dupey, if he could wait at our house for the delivery to arrive.

He got to our house HOURS before they were scheduled to arrive because a) he was always so early for everything – he didn't know how to be late, and b) he was just so excited to be a part of the day. While I don't know for sure, I can bet that he asked the delivery crew tons of questions. How was the table built? What kind of wood was the table made from? How should the table be cleaned? What is your social security number? (Well, maybe not that one.) I also can bet that he told the crew how they could do their job better and swore under his breath as they parked wrong, unwrapped wrong and finagled through the door wrong. The poor delivery guys. They probably couldn't get out of our house fast enough.

Usher Dupey couldn't wait for us to get home that night so he could come over again and make sure that everything was okay with the table. (It was as if he built it himself.) He gave us the slip that he signed confirming the order. I'm sure that, to him, his signature was as important as those on the Declaration of Independence. I saved the slip. I love seeing his name in his writing.

Man, I sure do miss him.

TRUTH

We got an email yesterday about a high school orientation meeting for parents next week. My heart nearly skipped a beat. How can this be? Aren't these babes o' ours just barely three?

I started talking to the girls about their first year of pre-school when they both, but especially Hannah, loooooooooooved their mumma. It was a big cry-fest every Tuesday and Thursday morning. Guy did not envy me at all at drop off. He still talks about how happy he was to be safe and sound in his office, away from the madness each week.

I remember (on more than one occasion) hearing my phone ring only minutes after dropping them off at pre-school. On the other line was one of their teachers. "Um…we THINK that Hannah is saying 'Sippy! Sippy!' Could you, please, maybe just drive it over here and put in on the desk in the outside hallway. BUT DON'T LET HER SEE YOU!! We think that may calm her down a bit."

I remember being so happy that their first class was so small. Two teachers for only eight kids. But the way it worked out (no joke) was one teacher for Hannah and another teacher for the other seven. One teacher had to manage seven coo coo two-year-olds so that the other one could manage our slubbering, blubbering two-year-old who needed her stinkin' sippy cup.

I remember the teachers doing backflips trying to keep her occupied each day as I left.

I remember seeing their faces as we walked in. "Oh, God. We hoped they (and by 'they' we mean Hannah) were sick today…"

I remember it as if it were yesterday. And now, they are heading off to high school. I just can't believe it.

I guess what I'm trying to say is, pre-school teachers don't get paid enough.

You thought I was going to say something sentimental, didn't you?

"THANK YOU, EASTER BUNNY. BOK BOK!!"

This morning, I was super cranky on my run. Silly me. I was dressed for May, because it is April but it felt like January. I was freezing. And did I mention I was crabby?

As I was nearly done, I ran by the house of a Forever Friend. The house of Forever Friends, really. Their dad was planting daffodils. Beautiful, bright yellow daffodils. They struck me because they were so warm and spring-y. Even though it felt like frickin' winter all over again.

I, of course, stopped to chat because a) I love to chat and b) I love this man.

We only spent about five minutes together. But in those five minutes, my entire perspective of my run changed. Hell – my entire perspective on a whole lot of things changed.

We talked about so many things – from Jesus to "Scarecrow" in The Wizard of Oz. (Don't ask. You had to be there.)

In those five minutes, we had some super serious moments. (I waited to cry until I ran away.)
In those five minutes, we had some super silly moments. (I cried from laughing at this guy. OMG - he is so funny and he has no idea.)

I spent the entire day (and more) thinking of his words.

Life is funny. You just need to keep your eyes and ears open. It's easy to miss life's blessings because you're not paying attention. They come when you least expect it.

Today, I was blessed to spend a few minutes with a dear, dear man. He let me see my many, many things more clearly.

An early Easter present. Lucky, lucky me.

NAME THAT TUNE

Earlier today, Maddie asked me, "Mumma, what's that song? You know. Something, something state of mind." As the breath returned to my body (I couldn't BELIEVE that she didn't have THAT Billy Joel song, of all his songs, right at the tip of her tongue…!!!), it occurred to me that there are countless "classic" songs that Hannah and Maddie probably don't know. Countless songs that they never will know – unless we introduce them.

Sure, they'll be fine without knowing these songs. But won't they be better if they know them?!? I mean, look how WE turned out!!

Here's my list of songs that I will be sure everyone in our Four Family is able to sing (and be happy about it) at the top of our lungs.

1. "New York State of Mind" – Billy Joel
2. "Sir Duke" – Stevie Wonder
3. "You've Got a Friend" – James Taylor
4. "Runaway" – Bon Jovi
5. "So Far Away" – Carole King
6. "Domino" – Van Morrison
7. "Hit Me With Your Best Shot" – Pat Benatar
8. "Here Comes the Sun" – The Beatles
9. "Crazy Train" – Ozzy Osbourne

(I'm not listing 10 songs. Only 9. Just because I can. It's my book, after all…)

Lessons start tomorrow morning at 10 a.m. Anyone want to tag along? Be my guest. I'll bring the wine and cheese.

LET'S START AT THE VERY BEGINNING

We were in the auditorium at St. Mary School. It was 1982. Miss Tucker told us that we were going to take a break from practicing the musical, "Barbeque for Ben." She was very excited because the boy who was going to play Ben was coming to rehearsal that day.

I don't remember for certain, but I'm pretty sure there were lots of giggles that followed. To a roomful of ten-year-old girls, the mere mention of a boy made us laugh.

He was wearing a football jersey and jeans. High tops too.

He walked down the steps on the far side of the room, while I sat in a chair in front of Miss Tucker's piano.

We rehearsed, all together, for an hour or so. We never said a word to each other. I'm pretty sure he didn't talk to anyone. He was twelve and probably only agreed to be in the play because he was asked to be in it and his mom told him that it was the right thing to do. He "should have been honored to have been asked. Everyone else had to audition." (I never actually heard her say those words, but in my head, I can.)

**

We were in the cafeteria at the Horace Mann Middle School. It was 1984. I was in sixth grade, he was in eighth. I'm not sure if we had assigned tables, but I do know that we typically sat directly behind each other.

That day, I had a juice box. He finished talking to his buddies and turned around to talk to me.
He seemed like a nice kid.

He told me to do it. I wasn't one to give in to peer pressure. But he was in eighth grade, remember? I was going to do what he told me to do. (Remember Maddie and Hannah. Do as I say, not as I do…)

So I did. Yep. I blew right in to the juice box and then peered in to the straw for something really cool to happen. (I mean, he told me to do it, after all.) Well, the only really cool thing that happened was that I was suddenly covered in juice. Dripping down my face. Yep. I don't remember what happened after that, but I'm pretty sure he made fun of me. And I'm pretty sure that I was annoyed and embarrassed. But secretly, I was probably a little bit happy too. The kid was sorta cute.

**

And now, decades later, he still makes fun of me. And he still wears football jerseys. And he still looks really good in jeans. And he still sometimes makes me so mad I could scream. And he still makes me laugh like no one else.

And I'd still not want it any other way.

PAR-TAY

I just picked up the bouncy house for the girls' birthday. Now to keep it a secret until Sunday.

What is it with me and surprises? I don't like to be surprised all that much myself. I have no idea why I am entirely obsessed with surprising Hannah and Maddie with so many things.

I am loving the girls' birthday deets this year. They will be 11 on 11/11. At 11:20 and 11:22. Too bad it's not 2011. (Poor planning on our part...)

They have rehearsals on Sunday, so before and after, some FSPA buddies will come over. They really don't have anything "birthday-ish" planned. It's not really a birthday party. They've never been big fans of birthday parties – either having them or going to them. They proclaimed once, in first grade or so, that they really weren't big fans of having a big party. It didn't take much to convince us. Money saved. Thanks, ladies!

Sunday will be no different than any other day. (Well, with the exception of the bouncy house. We don't typically have that parked out back.) They will sing, dance, make countless music videos and short movies. They will eat and bounce and sing and bounce and eat and dance and bounce and sing. And bounce.

It's sure to be the easiest, no frills birthday ever. We won't really even see them except when we have to drive them to and from FSPA. "Mom and dad, who?!?!" (But isn't that what 11 is all about anyway?)

I love that they don't feel like we have to make a big deal about their birthday. I'd like to think it's because every day feels like a party in some way.

Now pass the onion dip and grab me a lemonade, *por favor*.

MUSIC TO MY EARS

This morning, as I was driving the girls to school, I was flipping through the radio stations and bumped into a current "hurts-your-ears-it's-so-bad-and-the-lyrics-and-melodies-are-so-repetitive-I-could-cry-and-my-four-year-old-students-could-do-better" pop music radio station. (I recognize that this statement makes me completely middle-aged and I think I'm okay with that...)

Anyhow, I overhead Hannah and Maddie talking in the backseat about how much they don't like [certain current music "stars'" music]. They apparently much prefer music that Guy and I (you know, us middle-aged types) listen to, like Stevie Wonder, Billy Joel, Elton John, Queen, Bon Jovi, and that "crazy train song that the guy with the eyes sings".

Brainwashing at its finest, folks. And for that, I make absolutely no apologies. A happy Mumma makes for a happy family.

GOOD MORNING, BALTIMORE...ER, FRANKLIN...

When I was a kid, my mom would wake me up slowly every morning by lifting my shades, quietly walking over to my bed, kissing me and whispering "Baby Kim, it's time to get up." She did this for as long as I can remember.

It was such a pleasant, peaceful way to start the day. No blaring alarm clock in my ear. (In fact, I don't think I ever used my alarm clock until I was in graduate school). No bright light in my face.

I think this wake-up call is one of the things that helped set the tone for the rest of the day. For the most part, I had nothing to complain about as a kid (heck, I still don't as an adult) and I'm pretty sure that I left the house each morning (okay, most mornings) with a smile on my face because of this gentle ease-in to the day.

Now, with Hannah and Maddie, I try to help them start the day the same way. Each school morning, they wake up before me and they come into our bedroom. They kiss me on the cheek and we cuddle in bed. Hannah with her Taggie in hand, squeezes in to my right side with my arm around her. Maddie wraps around under my left arm, curled into a little ball squeezing out as many moments of quiet as she can muster.

Most mornings we don't talk. If we do, it's usually about any dreams they had, what the day ahead of us looks like. Little things. Mostly we just chill. We hardly ever fall asleep. Unless it's a weekend and then all bets are off.

Depending on what time our cuddle time starts, we stay there for five, ten, or twenty minutes. (That's my favorite option...) Then, I head downstairs to throw together a quick breakfast while they grab the last few minutes of cuddle time. I often wonder if they chat or just chill. Either way, I love the thought of them sharing those few minutes together each day. Sometimes, as I leave the room, I hear little giggles or pushes and shoves, as they jockey to the right positions.

Today's breakfast was strawberries (mother of the year award) and left over Chinese chicken fingers (mother of the year award goes to someone else). In our house, you must have a healthy breakfast. However, that healthy breakfast may also include Chinese leftovers, cold pizza or Fruity Pebbles whenever possible.

Maddie and Hannah are happy kids. That's pretty darn clear.
Is it because of our morning routine? Probably not. But I'm not willing to give it up. Just in case.

SAY CHEESE

I sometimes have my students play a game where I show them a picture and then I ask them to come up with a name or a caption for the picture.

If I were playing this game, my answers for this picture would be:

Don't Let Life Get in the Way of Life

Making Lemonade Out of Lemons

Live Life to the Fullest

Don't Be Fooled. Things Suck More Than They Appear

Surround Yourself with Love

Surround Yourself with My Mother

SECOND DAY OF ZERO

Yesterday was my birthday. I am now officially 44.
Today is my second day of 44.

My first day of 44 rocked it.
I cooked and I ran. Two of my favorite things to do – and incidentally, I do a lot of the former which is why I must do a whole bunch of the latter.

We had a house full of family and friends for New Year's Day (which happens to be my birthday.)
Love.
I laughed and hugged all day long.

The Village that I call mine blesses me beyond measure. I never take this or them for granted.
Pinky swear.

But really, yesterday, my first day of 44 rocked because Eleanor Rose, my cousin, was born.
She is delicious in every way and has two of the best peeps for parents, my cousins, you could ever ask for. Like, if you wished, hoped, planned, prayed for parents, you'd want these two to be your parents.

I can't wait to meet her.
I can't wait to kiss off her face.

She is named after my Auntie Ellie, my cousin's Nonnie and, for that reason alone, she is destined to have the biggest heart in the land.
This also means that she is destined to have the best lipstick and biggest glasses in the land as well.
But we need to give her some time.
It's only her second day of zero. She needs some time to acclimate.

And on this, her second day of zero, I pledge to make this world a better place for Ellie.
In my own little way.
By loving on her and making sure that she knows how much we love her.
'Cuz, no joke, I love her so much, my heart hurts.

IS THAT ME?

Have you ever looked at yourself as you walked by a mirror and were surprised at what you saw? That just happened to me.

I'm wearing an outfit that is so "not me" today. My hair, my necklace, my shoes, my skirt. I obviously put it on myself but it surprised me.

It made me wonder how other people see me. And hear me. I'd love to get a glimpse of myself, but not as me looking at myself but as somebody else looking at myself. Get it? I bet it's totally different than how I see myself. I don't know if that's a good thing or a bad thing.

I doesn't much matter, I guess. It is what it is. I think I'm quite lovely. In my own mind. I guess I'd like to keep thinking that's how others see me too.

LET'S (NOT) MAKE MUSIC

A few days ago, at FPAC's *Les Misérables* auditions, I reconnected with Hannah and Maddie's first music teacher. Miss Chrissy was adorable in every way. We chatted for a bit and she was saying how cute they were when they were little. I reminded her that it was a good thing they were cute because they were so horribly behaved in that class. Miss Chrissy said she didn't remember that about them. Miss Chrissy is still adorable but – she also lies.

They were maybe two. Adorable. Little itty bitties. Coordinated outfits (sort of like the Mandrell sisters but only two of them). Massive heads of great hair. Ponytails on the tops of their heads. Chubby cheeks. Little hands, little feet. But also, BIG voices CRYING, incessantly. The. Entire. Time. In. Miss. Chrissy's. Class. Every. Single. Stinkin'. Week.

It was a "mommy and me"-type class. Truthfully, not my cup of tea, but I understand why some folks like that class dynamic. As such, I sat right next to both of them. For the entire class. They couldn't have possibly been closer to me and yet, they never stopped crying. From the moment we walked in until the moment we walked out.

Every mom and EVERY OTHER CHILD loved the class. How could they not? It had drums, bells, scarves, triangles, puppets, guitars, hula-hoops. And my loser children. Crying. Non-stop. We'd get up from the floor and walk around the room and they'd cling to my leg and start to sweat with stress. And then, I'd start to sweat with stress.

I tried to imagine that they were not there with me. I tried to imagine that they belonged to someone else. Some other mother of loser children. It was painful. But alas, they were mine. All mine.

I'm pretty sure that the other moms cringed each week as we walked in. They surely hoped we'd be absent. I'm pretty sure that I got "the look" from them whenever we walked through the door. That was fun. And yet I was determined to make it work. And I did. I bribed them. With candy. I'm not proud. But it worked. Eventually.

I still can't figure out why they were so miserable in the class. The class was fabulous. Miss Chrissy was fabulous. It was just my children. They sucked.

Oh, man, they sucked so bad.
Dammit. I'm starting to sweat again just thinking about it.

CRASH, BOOM, BANG!!!

It's as if I unexpectedly and suddenly have a teenager in the house. A teenager who is going through a mid-life crisis.

And to make this whole thing even better (and by that I mean the opposite of better) is that the mid-life crisis teenager in my house suddenly plays the drums.

I called Guy's cell last night to see if he was home and able to meet us out for dinner. No answer.

Oh, right. He was practicing on his new (and first ever) drum set in our cellar and couldn't hear the phone ring.

To his credit, I totally recognized the song that he was playing. Particularly, considering he's only been playing the drums for 2.8 days, I have to say that I'm pretty darn impressed with his drumability. Drumbility. Drumility? (One of these should totally be a word, if you ask me.)

Of course, this is all still a new and fun idea. Talk to me in six months and he may be playing the drums on the sidewalk. Across town.

SIBS AND SOX

My aunt (mom's sister/my godmother) is visiting for a few days from North Carolina. She and my uncle (mom's brother) made a bet early this summer, that if the Sox made it to the World Series, she would travel up from NC to MA and they would go to a game together. Neither one of them wanted to jinx anything, so I don't think they talked much about the bet after their initial conversation. The Sox are trailing 1-0 as I write. I hope they win. My uncle is a bit of a freak (I mean that in the nicest way possible) when it comes to baseball stats and thinking of him in the stands with his sister makes me smile.

Before they left for the game, they met up with my mom and me for lunch. Three siblings (and me) that, in many ways, couldn't possibly be more different from each other. And yet, three siblings that, when together, are so awesome. Simply seeing them together makes me smile. Honestly, my stomach hurt from laughing at them. It was awesome.

A few months ago, to say that we didn't think that the Sox would be in the World Series is an understatement.

A few months ago, to say that we didn't think my mom would be out to lunch with us like that is an even bigger understatement.

After my mom's accident, Hannah and Maddie's very first thought was "Will Nonie be able to teach us how to cook ever again?" (Yes, they both asked it simultaneously when we first told them about my mom's accident.) My first thought was "Will she ever be able to climb the steps to see the girls play in a piano recital again?" My second thought was, "Will we ever be able to go out to dinner easily again?" It's funny. We are definitely more of a "hang in/cook for friends and family" kind of crew as opposed to a "go out to dinner" gang, but still it was that thought that initially struck me.

And yet, only two months later, after easily the worst day of our lives, my mom is rocking the world – walking, working, driving, going out - and cooking.

Life's not the same as it was. But it is pretty close. I guess she'd beg to differ, but it's fair to say that it's much closer than we thought it would ever be again. And for that, I'm thankful.

Go Sox!

CHOICES

This morning, I sang and played at a funeral for a 23-year-old boy who died of a drug overdose.

I knew a few folks in the congregation and, of course, I know many people his age, just out of college-age, trying to figure out who, what and why they are.

Although I didn't know this kid at all, I had a really difficult time getting through the Mass. It was all I could do to not start bawling uncontrollably, thinking about the many "kids" in my life, and I said a special prayer for them. If I could have wrapped them all up in my arms at that very moment just to let them know that they were respected and loved, I would have.

And, of course, I also thought about Maddie and Hannah. Right now, if they make a "bad choice" it usually consists of hip-checking the sister as they walk up the steps or telling me that they've put their cup in the dishwasher when, in reality, it's still on their bureau.

Big deal, right?

These choices, I can live with. We all can.

But, as a parent, how do you live each day, not knowing whether or not your kid is going to make that one wrong choice that starts the spiral of a lifetime of bad choices? Forever.

Oh my God, I think I'll be on the verge of crying all day.

...RIBBIT...

Today, at an allergist appointment (dead end, got me nowhere), I was cracking jokes with the little old man who sat next to me in the waiting room. I was hysterical. The old-ish ladies behind the desk were cracking up. I was on fire. (Dammit. If only I'd put out a tip jar, I bet I could have made some extra spending money.)

Then, when I went in the room, the nurse came in and I carried on with her like we were BFFs. She wasn't as old as Johnny in the Lobby but she was still decades older than me. I'm pretty sure she came just short of asking me if I wanted to go out for lunch.

When the young, handsome doctor came in, I had nothing to say. Nothing. In fact, I wasn't even able to talk to him about why I was there. I was speechless. Not funny. Not clever. Not even remotely entertaining.

I am really funny if my audience is 75 and older or 4 and younger. If you are between the ages of 4 and 75, I am simply taking up space in your world.

You know that frog in Looney Tunes that dances with the hat and cane when no one is looking but just sits like a bump on a log when someone's paying attention to him? Yep – that's pretty much me.

DID I REALLY JUST SAY THAT?!

As I ran by the street where two of my best friends grew up, I recalled this day. And I giggled for the rest of the day. And then some.

We were in high school, I think. Maybe college. Alyssa Jane, one of my BFFs, and I were in the backseat of the car. Her parents were in the front. We were getting ice cream.

I had weird ways of saying things at the time. (I still do.) I don't remember exactly what we were talking about, but I know that I ended my sentence with "Oh, happiness." And I think I must have, sort of, run out of breath as I said it.

Alyssa Jane's mom asked me what I said and my response was "Oh, I said 'hap' and then I just squeezed out the 'ppiness'".

We were all silent for a minute. And then we all burst out laughing.

Don't get it?
Say it out again. Out loud. You will.

THE MYSTERY TF VISIT

One day, in second grade or so, Hannah lost her tooth in school. She was thrilled because she had a dentist appointment later that day and she was terrified that they would pull out the tooth if it didn't fall out of its own accord.

When we got home from the dentist, she went upstairs to change. On her bed, she found a great pair of red and white striped socks with penguins on them. Right up her alley. "Wow! The Tooth Fairy already came!!" She looked at Maddie with delight and amazement and Maddie did the same. They ran downstairs to see if Hannah's tooth was still in the envelope that they had given her in school. It was not there.

Now – there was my conundrum. I had NO idea where the socks came from. But, no one else knew that Hannah's tooth had come out yet and, even if they did, no one in our world would only bring Hannah a gift and not Maddie. Tooth or not.

Should I continue with their belief that the TF had visited early? What if I decided to not put anything under her pillow that night, she realized that the socks were from someone else and then she was devastated that the TF actually never came. What if the envelope with the tooth showed up eventually? Did they look really well for it in her backpack? Oh God.

That night, I decided to play it safe and gave her a little something from the TF. I didn't have a chance to run out to buy anything so I put $2 under her pillow. When she woke up the next morning, I asked her if anything was left under her pillow. She told me that she hadn't even bothered looking because she was sure that the TF was responsible for the socks. "Just to be sure", she went upstairs, found the cold hard cash, shared none with her sister and put the socks on for the day. Life was good.

I still have no stinkin' idea where the damn socks came from. Maybe there really IS a Tooth Fairy. I mean, could there be any other explanation?!?!

BITS AND PIECES

As I was running this morning, I was going through the day's events. Tonight, we will go to watch Guy's softball game. As an aside, he refuses to believe that I was (once) a pretty good softball player as a kid. I played short stop and second base on all-star teams. I batted fourth. What else does he need to know??! I'm sure a lot of folks are surprised by this fact. My sports prowess (other than running, I guess) clearly maxed out when I was twelve.

There are probably lots of things about me that may surprise you:

I can name an embarrassing number of WWF wrestlers from the 1980's.

I only eat certain foods, like grapes, crackers and cookies in multiples of two. Similarly, I also only buy certain foods, like cans of corn, boxes of mac and cheese and flavored water in multiples of two. Must be a twin thing.

I become inexplicably nervous when I have to make coffee (in something other than a one-serving machine.)

I am equally unnerved when I have to drive when other adults are in the car.

It would take a lot to make me leave my house in the morning with our bed unmade or dishes in the sink.

If I could dress every day like one person or character from the movies or TV, it would be Natalie Portman's character in "Mr. Magorium's Wonder Emporium".

Dirty feet nauseate me. So do dirty finger nails and runny noses. (I guess, who isn't nauseated by these things but being a teacher of young children, I am faced with this more than most.)

One of my favorite movies is "Mommy Dearest". Don't judge.

I haven't thrown up since I was nine.

New office supplies make me so happy. Especially those pointy erasers that you put on the ends of pencils.

The idea of getting dressed up in a costume for Halloween makes me suddenly feel "sick and unable to attend the party, but have fun everyone."

Other than during my driving lesson, I've never parallel parked. I can't. I won't. I will drive and drive for blocks until I have a spot that doesn't require it.

In high school, I truly wanted my husband to be in the Mafia. Thankfully, I changed my mind.

I have never, not even once, wished we'd had another baby after Hannah and Maddie.

I've never gone on a job interview or needed a resume. Here's hoping I never will.

TO HAVE AND TO HOLD

Over forty years ago, the stars were aligned, the world was forever changed, and (my) life began.

It actually happened years before that. I don't even know how old they were when they first met. Junior high? I totally should know. I'll have to ask one of their best friends – who remembers everything – and who was probably there when they met.

September 24, 1971. The day my mom and dad got hitched. He was 20. She was 18. Babes.

One of my favorite stories is when my dad learned who my mom's father was. "Your dad is the guy who works down the alleys?!" "Yes, why?" "Oh, no reason." But I'm sure his face said it all. He had given my grandfather (and countless others) grief for years at the alleys, pushing the envelope "just enough". Not enough to really get in trouble but enough to be an ongoing pain in the ass. (They say that you marry someone like your father. Um, yep.)

They were so young when I was born. Most of their friends didn't have children for years. For this reason (and maybe because I was an only child) I spent a lot of time with my parents and their friends while I was growing up. My relationships with their besties have had a lot to do with who I have become today.

My parents are still friends with nearly everyone who was in their lives back then. This, I think, speaks to the incredible people that they are. If you are no longer in their lives, for whatever reason, I feel sad for you. They simply make people's lives happy.

Their loyalty to their family and friends is unprecedented. Their loyalty to each other is greater.

For as long as I can remember, they have taught me how to be married. Good, bad, and otherwise, these two know how to do it. No one is perfect (although I certainly proclaim to be). No one is right all the time (see previous statement). But they have figured it out. I hope that Guy and I teach Maddie and Hannah as much as my parents have taught us about being a couple. Husband and wife. Friends.

Sure, they've been thrown some curveballs. A big one of epic proportion recently. But true to form, they are figuring it out. Together.

Happy Anniversary to the best of the best. For reals.

Love,
Your Favorite Daughter

THEIR WORLD

Sometimes, they wrap themselves up in each other's arms like they are one person.
Especially at night when they are asleep.
They start in different beds, but often, they end up in one.
It's something I can't explain.
It's something I don't understand.
I marvel at it.
I could watch them like this for hours.
It's something special that only people who have shared a belly for months can understand.

They get it.
We don't.
And we never will.

SEASONS OF LOVE

As much as I'd love to live in the "perfect" climate 365 days a year, as I was running this morning, I was thinking of all the things that I love about New England. Sure, a lot of these seasonal things happen elsewhere. It's just that they can all happen here in the course of approximately four days!! Plus, I don't think I'd appreciate any of them as much if I had any of them year-round. As much as I enjoy each season, I'm always happy to see the next one 'round the bend.

WINTER
The first snowfall of the season
My kids' red cheeks after playing outside in the snow
Those really big snowflakes that are so big you are convinced they must be fake
When you leave yourself enough time to fully defrost your car so you don't need to scrape
The sound of the heat coming from the radiators
An unexpected snow day
Those last few minutes of a warm cuddle before you start the day
Listening to Maddie and Hannah count the snowflakes on their tongues (may they never be too old to do this)
Not having to worry about ticks or sunburns
When you've run far enough that you can take off your gloves because you're sweating
Finding animal tracks in the snow
Listening to Hannah, Maddie and Guy share their sledding stories with me. (I don't like winter enough to go sledding…)

SPRING
Running in a warm rain
Opening up our windows for the first time
Jeans and flip-flops
Realizing that there is no more salt or sand marks on my floor
The sound of snow melting from the roof of the house
Seeing all the local runners on the street the few days after Marathon Monday.
The smell of new mulch
The smell of rain
When flowers and plants start to poke through the ground
Running out the door without a jacket
Running in shorts

Counting down the days until

SUMMER
The perfect beach day
Heads of hair, sticky with sand and sunblock
Watching the Red Sox on TV, knowing that so many other people are doing the same
Walking into a nice cool centrally air-conditioned house after a day of too much heat
Daytime thunderstorms
Cheeseburgers on the grill
Listening to the waves
Fireflies and butterflies
Watching and listening to the girls and Guy play softball in the backyard

FALL
When Hannah and Maddie come inside and they "smell like fall" (I can't explain it but if you know what I'm talking about, am I right or am I right?)
Shorts and sweatshirts
Pumpkins, apple crisp and hayrides
Chili, cornbread and red sauce
Fire pits
Listening to Maddie and Hannah when they can see their breath for the first time of the season
Needing a blanket to watch TV
Realizing you have stopped having to argue nightly with mosquitos
How nice our yard looks after it's been raked (only to have to rake it again three days later)

Truth be told, right now, I'm pretty much done with winter. But in reality, we still have months to go! We'll make it through. We always do. And next year, at this time, we'll do it all over again (as my Gram would say), "God willing."

FIVE MEN

I have a photograph on our fridge of five men. Five great men. Two of them are my grandfather/Usher Dupey and Uncle Louie and the other three are "townies", men whose families my family has known for years, decades, lifetimes. These men depict to me a number of things, among them – Faith, Family, Friends, Community and Love.

I don't know exactly when the photo was taken, but I think it was late 60's/early 70's. The Five Men are at the Knights of Columbus annual Pancake Breakfast. They are stationed behind two griddles making pancakes.

Two of the Four (my Usher Dupey and Uncle Louie) are cracking up, having a grand ol' time, with pancake batter dripping off the sides of the griddle, pancakes half-flipped, haphazardly on their sides. The others are, well, um, let's just say that they are taking this pancake breakfast much more seriously. They are peering at the other two, very much with a, "hey guys, this is a very serious event here, let's get this right." Their griddle is spotless with each pancake symmetrically identical to the others. As I look at the picture, I can read the mind of all Five Men, even though I only really knew two (the more serious of the two) very well.

This morning, the last of the Five passed away. (He is one of the haphazard griddlers.) Now, the Five Men are gone. That makes me so sad. As much as I love the generation of which I am a part, I really believe that they simply don't make 'em like they used to. Of course, there are exceptions and I am truly blessed to have many of these exceptions in my world.

But still, I ran today and felt sad for Maddie and Hannah. They have more people in their lives that love them to the moon and back than most people could ever dream of. I know this to be true.

And yet I can't help but hope and pray that they have Five Men in their lives that they recognize, appreciate and cherish, to always remind them that there is good in this world. And that there always will be.

THE MORE THINGS CHANGE

I am sitting at my desk as the seven Von Trapp children get fitted in their costumes for the Franklin Performing Arts Company's upcoming production of "The Sound of Music."

Major déjà vu. I was cast as Gretl in the St. Mary production many moons ago. I guess it would have been March, 1984. All I know is I was twelve but easily passed for seven, tops.

I remember practicing my audition song in Raye Lynn's living room (well, I guess it was Dr. and Mrs. Mercer's living room at the time) as if it was yesterday. Tonight, she is down the hall, not as the pianist as she was many years ago, but as the director. I am so very much in awe of all that she does.

The woman who played Liesl to my Gretl now works here too.

The guy who played Friedrich is now my brother-in-law.

Small, small world, huh?

SAY WHAT??!

I am good at many things. I know this to be true.

I also am not so good at many things. And I am okay with this. Really.

Among the things that I am good at, dealing with and being with young children is at the top of my list. I am, to them, hysterical, comforting, goofy, understanding, empathetic, sympathetic, smart and witty. (Even though they don't know what these words mean, I am definitely these things to them.) I understand little kids. And they understand me. I'm not being conceited. It's where I really find myself thinking "well then, nice work, kid."

I will tell you a circumstance where I do not, under any circumstance think to myself "nice work, kid." In fact, it is in these instances where I think the exact opposite. It is in these instances where I, instead, think, "for the love of God, kid, stop. Just stop. Stop the madness before someone gets hurt."

I am talking about when I am in a room full of pre-teens or teens.

I am (sometimes) okay in one-on-one conversations with said double-digit aged beings. I can converse with them and be marginally successful. But get me in a classroom or group of said beings and I may as well be living on the moon. Unlike what I said above, I don't understand them and they sure don't understand me. I don't understand how they talk. Or dress. Or smell. I don't understand how they walk or think or, quite simply, exist. I don't understand anything about them.

I'm fairly positive they say the same about me.

I have tried for many years.

I recently saw someone whom I knew when he was a teenager. He is now a grown adult, married man with three adorable children. I hadn't seen him in years and our conversation started with my saying "You probably don't remember me but..." His response was "Oh, I totally remember you. I had a crush on you when I was in high school." Well, I burst out laughing. That's probably not the response he was hoping or thinking he'd get, but I just find it shocking that any teen (boy or girl) would find me anything other than annoying, stupid, and, have I mentioned annoying? Really. I was deeply flattered by his honesty. But I question his judgement!!

Now, I find myself raising and being responsible for two teenaged daughters.

I can't imagine this is going to end well. For any of us.

POWER OF TWO

In my self-induced insomnia last night/this morning, (who knew how much caffeine was in a black iced coffee??!?!), I rediscovered the song "Power of Two" by the Indigo Girls.

It clearly was not written (I wouldn't imagine) about two sisters. But in my world, when I first heard it, Maddie and Hannah were just babies and it struck a chord with me. I am now obsessed with it again and I listened to it over – and over – and over again this morning on my run.

At some point in their FSPA lives, they must sing this song. I'll be the mother blubbering in the corner.

THREE WORDS

Last week, Guy and I were on vacation. We were sitting at The Beach Bar (have I mentioned how much we love St. John?) and there were little boxes that had "Conversation Starters" in them. Now, it's pretty crystal clear that, quite typically, neither one of us need help in the "talking" department, but we decided to play. It was fun.

"What do you love most about your hometown?"
"If you could be sure that you would not be harmed in any way, would you rather skydive or dive with sharks?"
"If you could meet anyone, past, present or future, who would you want to meet?"
"What three words do you think your family would use to describe you?"
And so on…

Um, what? Back up. What's that last one again?

That one threw me for a loop.

I never really thought about that before. And it made me think a LOT (I had a LOT of glorious free time on the beach) about what other people think of me.

When it comes right down to it, I have no idea how others see me. What three words WOULD they use to describe me? That's crazy to think about!

What if how I think other people see me is ENTIRELY different from how they REALLY see me?
What if I think I'm HYSTERICAL and they only can slightly tolerate me (with lots of wine nearby.)
What if I think that people are thrilled to see me when they are really searching for the nearest get-away?
What if I think my students love me but they really can't wait for their class to be over so they can go have some "real fun"?

Dammit. Damn you. Damn you, Conversation Starters.

A NEAR PERFECT CIRCLE

When I was pregnant with Hannah and Maddie, I was…well, let's just say…a bit less than gorgeous. I did not look even remotely like the supermodel-type pregnant people you see in magazines and on book covers. And I'm really okay with that. I had a lot going on that needed my attention. Well, maybe I'm a little bitter.

Guy went to every single doctor's appointment with me - even those that lasted less than five minutes. I had more appointments than most. Given our history (looooong story) he didn't want me to be alone. Ever. My husband rocked the "my wife is pregnant" world.

Anyway, at one such appointment, we were waiting for quite a while for the doctor to come in the room. We were bored and Guy saw that tape measure thingy on the counter. He thought it'd be funny to measure my belly – all the way around. (He's really quite like a young child stuck in an adult male body, but I digress.)

I was huge. Massive. No need to sugar coat it. Either now or then.

He started to measure me and he had to pull quite hard to fit all the way around my massive pre-natal orb. Suddenly, the tape measure broke.

It was at the exact moment when we realized that I was over 4 feet around. I am only 5 feet tall. (On a particularly tall day.)

I was a beach ball.
And for that visual, you're welcome.

APPLES AND ORANGES

During these three months, besides running a few miles here and there, I have:

...

...

um ... well, I ... ahhh ...
Oh right, remember that time when I ...?
... Wait a minute! I ......
And, of course, there was the time when I ... um ...
Well, I'm pretty sure that I did that thing with the ...

So, I guess, come to think of it, I've not done much with myself over these ninety days.

However, during this time, my mom has been through a lot. Sometimes I forget because she's just THAT amazing

She doesn't listen to anyone who tells her that she "can't", "may not be able to", "I don't know if" or "I don't think you're ready to."

She is determined each day to do something that she's not been able to do the day before. She continues to "wow" her therapists, doctors and nurses each and every day and we have been told by her surgeon and neurologist (more than once) that she is a "miracle."

Yup, I just said that.

She is walking, driving, cooking and working. Oh, and last night, she and my dad went to a work-thing for my dad in Boston and, she um, ... she um, danced.

Yup, I just said that.

That's what she's done in three months.

I am a loser.
She is a-ma-zing.

Yup, I just said that.

MEA CULPA

When hanging up the phone with the girls, Guy or my parents, I ALWAYS say "'kay, I love you, bye". I don't even think about it. I just say it.

The other day, I was on the phone with a FSPA dad. His son and daughter have been students of ours forever. He's super great. His wife is super great. Their kids are super great. Love.

I was hanging up from the phone with him and – yep, you guessed it. I said to him, under no uncertain terms, ""'kay, I love you, bye". And then we hung up.

I nearly died.

I called him right back and told him that, while I do think he is great, I don't like him THAT way.

I wish I could have seen his face as we hung up.
I wish he could have seen MY face as we hung up.

...that's one way to get more students, I s'pose...

Good grief.

STAR MAIL

The girls and I were in my office. We were talking about the previous weekend and "The Sound of Music" production they were in. Hannah and I were chatting and Maddie yelled out, "Oh, Mumma, guess what?!?! Guess who we got a Star Mail from yesterday??!!!"

Star Mail is a great thing where patrons can send a "break a leg/great job" message to a Franklin Performing Arts Company performer backstage. Sometimes cast members will send to each other as well. You put the message in a big mailbox and it gets sent backstage during intermission. It's so much fun and a great way for performers to get pumped for their performance while our Company can raise a little bit of money too.

Anyway, after numerous (failed) attempts at guessing, Maddie told me that the Star Mail was from Mairead (a girl who played a lead Von Trapp role).

"Oh, how nice. She seems like a total cutie patootie. I'm happy that you're becoming friendly with her."

"But, Mumma, why would SHE give US one? She's a LEAD and we're only in the ENSEMBLE!!!"

Time for Life Lesson #396

I am very thankful to Mairead for unknowingly giving us that quick opportunity to chat about life at that moment.

Sometimes when you least expect it, you can teach your kids something really important.

(Side note: four years later and Hannah, Maddie and Mairead are total BFF's. Love.)

THANK YOU

To all the amazing dads in my life –

Thank you for being such great dads. It's not an easy job. (Largely because you have to deal with us moms.)

Thank you for keeping us safe and protected.

Thank you for all the things you don't say, even though you want to, because you know that is usually the wisest choice. (You've learned well over the years.)

Thank you for doing all that you can to give us all that we need and then some.

Thank you for doing things for us when you'd rather be doing things for yourselves, all the while (or at least most of the time) with smiles on your faces.

Thank you for making us laugh when we really want to cry.

Thank you for making us laugh when we really want to scream.

Thank you for knowing when to "fix" and when to "listen".

Thank you for making it easier to be a mom because you are by our side.

Thank you. Thank you. Thank you.

A DAY IN THE LIFE

Some of my random thoughts from my run today, in no particular order.

Really, with a fanny pack, lady?

Ah, young love. Man, I am old.

How in the HELL are we going to pay for college???!!

I hope the people renting the Cape house this week use the s'mores stuff at least once.

Could Bradley Cooper be any cuter? I'm pretty sure he'd love me if he knew me.

I can't believe I can't find that lipstick. Where could I have left it?

Remember when Maddie and Hannah used to be attached at my hip? Now, it's all I can do to have them come visit me when they have a break between classes at FSPA. (Be careful what you wish for, I guess.)

Brillo pads are totally gross.

Should we book a dinner at Downtown Disney this year? Oh my God! Maddie was so crabby that last time we were there. She SO did not appreciate the three of us making fun of her. Ah well.

I really don't think it's necessary for me to pay attention to the "we are crashing" directions when I'm on a plane. If I ever find myself in that situation, I am going with my gut instinct.

My husband is in a band. Excuse me?

How many pens and pencils did I lose yesterday? Where did they go?

How do you tell someone that everything will be okay when, to them, it seems as if their entire world is falling apart?

I guess I should have applied a bit more sunblock.

Don't forget to call Nike and ask them why this app isn't working.

49 years old. Way too young and amazing to die. Horrifying.

That'll have to wait until tomorrow.

I wonder how many people have blocked me on Facebook. That's annoying.

How did I ever not like avocados or olives or mustard? Weirdo.

ARE YOUR EARS BURNING?

In a few hours, the girls' first friends, "The Boys" are coming over. We'll hang out with their parents all night, they'll play for hours – doing God knows what – and we'll all love every minute of it. We are not technically family but we go to each other's "family parties" year 'round so I guess that qualifies. We love them to pieces and we are so thankful that they are in our lives. I know they always will be.

It made me start to think of friends that I had when I was younger. Which made me think of people, in general, that were in my life when I was younger (many of whom I've not thought of in a long time.) Which made me wonder if any of them ever think of me. Which totally creeped me out.

Twins, Amy and Julie, were the first twins I ever knew. Had I known, I'd have paid more attention to them when I had them at my disposal every day for years! I remember them being so different from each other, in nearly every way. I wonder what they are up to now. They were super cute.

I dated a guy, Doug, who my cousins are still close to. I was a complete and total jerk to him. In every way. I honestly am still bothered by this. He was SUCH a nice guy and I was so, well, not nice to him. I hear that he is married so, thankfully, I did not turn him off from the entire female species. Phew.

I had a love/hate relationship with Chris. For the most part, I am not competitive, as an adult. I think that this is partly because I was off the charts competitive with Chris throughout all of elementary school. If he got 19 math problems right, I'd be damned if I wasn't going to get 20. If he skipped a reading level, I wouldn't rest until I did the same. Thinking of him reminds me that, at one point in my life, I was actually pretty smart. Not quite sure what happened…he probably owns Silicon Valley…

Mrs. Goss was the most beautiful teacher – person – in the world when I was in second grade. She looked just like Snow White. I saw her ten or fifteen years ago. I told her that she still looked like Snow White. That's sorta weird, I know, but she so does. I'm sure she thought that I was a freak.

I wonder if anyone is thinking about me right now. What are they thinking? Are they writing about me in THEIR book? Oh God. I need a drink.

PRESERVATION

Today, when I get home from my run, I plan on printing out all of my Facebook posts. I think it'd be funny to, someday, read all of them. Maddie and Hannah will surely be mortified but I guess we'll cross that bridge when we come to it.

I think that, ultimately, they will enjoy reading about themselves when they are older. When I am older. And in the horrible nursing home not far from our house. It's the most depressing place I've ever seen. Every time we drive by, Guy says "Everyone say 'hi' to Mumma." Seriously, if I ever end up in a place like that, I'll lose my mind.

He's such a jerk.

TOUCHES

Yesterday, we heard of a local family that is in the throes of an unspeakable tragedy. All day long, and still today, I have been a little bit off. Part of me is in absolute heartbreak mode for them, and the other part of me is in absolute take-my-breath-away-from-fear mode that I will lose a child as they just did. There are truly no words for that. They are, and forever will be, broken.

It made me think about the little touches in life that we are a part of each day, each week, each month that we don't really think about. Those little touches that truly affect us, in ways big and small, that we don't even realize. I'm not talking about the huge life-changing touches, and I'm not talking about the one and done touches. I'm talking about the day to day, week to week repeat touches that we live over and over again that are seemingly quite tiny compared to other bigger things in our lives. But really, when it comes right down to it, it's these little moments – these little touches – that fill our lives and get us from where we are to where we are going. They happen so quickly we often miss them.

I know that it's not always the biggest, loudest, earth-shattering moments that have the most impact on our lives.
I know that it's not always the biggest, loudest, earth-shattering people that have the most impact on our lives.
I know that it's the little things that, when put together, have a big, loud earth-shattering impact on us every day.

And I also know that I will miss his little peeks around the hallway door every Thursday afternoon. I will miss his little footsteps running down the hallway.

We may have not known him all that well.
But he touched us.
And we will miss his touches.

1300 MILES

You know when you walk into a house and it feels like home? I mean there are plenty of houses that I've been in where I feel completely comfortable. Like, I will open up their cabinets and pour myself a glass of wine-comfortable. That's a great feeling (especially if they have yummy wine). But what I'm talking about is when you are in a house that literally feels as if you are home. In your home. Even though you are not.

Well, that place for me (us) is far away from here. Like, 1300 miles away.

When we are there, Guy and I sleep in the "guest cottage" (I know that goes against my saying I feel as if it's my home, but anyway...) and the girls sleep in their own room in the house. They love the fact that they are in a different house than us.

Every time we visit, it is not long enough. It is not soon enough before our next visit.

Maddie and Hannah learned how to swim there. They learned how to knit there. They learned how to play Mexican Dominos. They learned how to make Christmas tags. They saw their first real and in person orange tree, and later that day, their first alligator (or was it a crocodile?!?!)

We eat delicious food, drink too much (well, some of us do) and we make extra batches of red sauce to be frozen for later. We tool around in a golf cart, laughing the entire time. We have celebrated La Befana (or as I call it "La Botswana") there and, because of our visits, we are now obsessed with visiting the "Sweet Tomato" (or as we call it in our house, the "Sweet To-MAH-to") every time we are there. We pile into the car with enough food and drink to visit Mickey for the day as if we're traveling to the other side of the world for a week instead of just a bit down the street.

On paper, there are four adults and two children in the car. But in our hearts, there are six children. Because the two oldest have taught us to live life to the fullest each and every minute. To laugh and to love. To giggle, squeal and fall on the floor with happiness. Literally.

You know those people that are in your life that you thank your lucky stars for? Well, the two people that live in the house that feels like our home are my "I thank my lucky stars for them" people. I honestly can't imagine life without them.

We share them with many (they are very, very popular...) and we are so very grateful for every minute that we get with them.

They have truly taught us (and many others) how to simply be. And for that, I am forever thankful.

We all are.

ONE LINERS

Taking two 10-year-olds back-to-school shopping requires a lot of patience, a sense of humor and alcohol.

Waking up your children every morning instead of letting them wake up to an alarm may lose you a few minutes of sleep each day, but you will start the first minutes of the day with a smile.

Hug your babies like you'll never let go.

If our daughters ever hang downtown with these kids, they will be grounded indefinitely. Additionally, Guy will have a heart attack and my dad and his best friend, Uncle Eddie, will rock-paper-scissors to see who will drive Maddie and Hannah to the convent.

If you are hanging up Christmas lights and have to maneuver around a scarecrow, rotten pumpkins or a bale of hay, you are either too early to deck the halls or terribly tardy in bringing autumn to a close.

I think that guy I bumped into yesterday was asking me out on a date. Little does he know that under this fleece jacket and running pants is a 40-year-old mother of twins.

Hmmm...I'm pretty sure that I just saw a lady running down 140 wearing leg warmers carrying a pizza box, chasing after a goose. You don't see that every day. (I can't make this stuff up, folks.)

Two sheep just ran alongside me for close to three minutes on Union Street. I am Laura Ingalls with an iPod and Nikes.

Why doesn't all of this running make me look like Heidi Klum?

I'm still unbelievably sad that Patrick Swayze died.

I am starving.

If today, I saw a picture of me the day before I die, would I recognize myself?

Wow. Ma'am, you really need to get your house power washed.

Oh my GAWD. I have not seen that kid in years. Age, you have not treated him well.

I would much rather be sleeping.

I would give anything to hold my grandfather's hand. Just one more time.

For the love of God, what the hell is that?!? Oh shit. Can I outrun a turkey?

Well, I'd say I just ran off two glasses of wine and a few pieces of cheese. Keep goin', kid!

WAIT, I HAVE ONE MORE THING TO SAY...

I didn't include "this" earlier in my book because I felt that by doing so, it would mean some sort of finality. But as this book became closer and closer to my reality, I realized that I had to. I had to sneak it in. How could I not share him with you? But, as I sit here and type, my fingers are having a hard time moving across the keys.

I've written about his sisters and I've written about his brothers-in-law. I've written about how much I miss them all and how much I'd give anything to spend even just five more minutes with them. I've written about how much being a part of his family means to me. His family is my family.

We are family. We are the Pecci family.

And he is one of the last Pecci's in my world. In fact, he is the last Pecci of his generation in my world. And there is truly no way I can tell you how that feels to me.

When I started writing this book, he was just as he always had been. Uncle Freddy - funny, quick witted, logical, clever, upbeat, perhaps a bit slower, but nonetheless, still charming, entertaining, jack-of-all-trades, gardener, jokester, plumber, electrician, carpenter, locksmith, fixer of all things.

I just wish he could fix this. But he can't. No one can. And it's breaking my heart. It's breaking lots of hearts.

I visited the other day and he didn't know who I was. He laughed as he told me that my "voice sounded familiar" but he couldn't quite place it. He said that I reminded him of "the girl who lives downstairs" (that's my cousin, so that sort of made sense) but still, have I mentioned he didn't know who I was? My Auntie Jan, who has been a rock star through all of this tried to explain to him, "Hun, she is Thelma and Louise's mom." (That's what he has always called Maddie and Hannah.) That didn't help. In fact, that probably made him more confused. But we laughed anyway. We laughed but it sucked.

It still sucks. And it will forever suck.

I want him to open up Fred's Shed one more time so he can host countless guys (no women allowed) on Saturday afternoons where they play cards, eat food, drink beer and wine like it's their business. I want him get razzed by so many (mostly my dad – like it's HIS business), say a 4:00 toast to Honk, and then get ready to do it all over again next week.

I want to be able to call him up and say "Uncle Freddy, our something-or-other is not working right. Can you come fix it?" And I want him to be there in under an hour to fix the something-or-other so that it's as if it was never broken.

I want to come home from a long day of work and find a big brown paper bag filled with his garden cucumbers, tomatoes, parsley, oregano, basil and, of course, hot peppers overflowing. And next to this bag, I want to see his handwritten note on a piece of paper towel in sharpie, telling him that he stopped by. (As if we'd ever mistake the delivery as being from anyone else.)

I want to visit his house on Halloween and see him in his front yard, all decked out from head to toe in costume, until the last trick-or-treater walks down the street. Music blaring, candy at the ready. Loving making people smile. Loving making people happy.

I want to see him walkaround the room (any room, as he did at our wedding) with a violin case filled with hot peppers for anyone brave enough to try. (He never played the violin, by the way…)

I want to be at a cookout with him as he secretly sneaks up to someone and starts scratching his/her neck with a long piece of grass, cracking up as he watches the unexpecting victim shoo away, what he/she thinks is an annoying fly or mosquito, for minutes on end. And then I want to watch Uncle Freddy simply walk away as he quietly finds someone else to bother.

I want to hear him tell stories of how he was the fastest runner on his baseball team. He has told me this for years, especially when I would tell him how much I love to run. "You might be able to run longer than I could but I bet I could run faster…" and, then, off he'd go on the story.

I want to hear him swear at my dad, I mean really swear at my dad. No one can piss off Uncle Freddy as much as my dad can. It's pretty much my dad's life mission. And yet, at the same time, I am convinced that my dad is like the son that my Uncle Freddy never had. And my Uncle Freddy is like the dad my dad never had.

I want to see him talk to my mom, with such love in his eyes, it hurts. And the love is felt in the other direction just the same. And then some.

I want him to know that my Auntie Jan, his wife, has never once complained about this shitty end of their life story. This is not how she had planned it. This is not how any of us had planned it. But she does everything that she can for him and never complains. Ever. And there's a lot to complain about right now. She doesn't even complain when he suddenly starts talking to her about "his wife" or "his wives" and how much he loves them and not her. I'm not sure if I'd be as strong as she is. She is the most appreciative person in the world when you do even the slightest thing to help her.

I want him to know how much I love him. How much we all love him. So, so many of us.

I want him to know how much I love that Hannah and Maddie have had him in their lives for so many years. I'm not sure how much longer they will have him but I cherish every minute. Every memory.

I want him to know how happy I am that he has been the last one to represent. The one to represent, for so long, the generation that was, still is and forever will be, so important to me. The one to represent unreal, awesome, unfathomable, unconditional love. Pecci Love. It's real. And it's fierce. And it's in my heart forever.

I want him to know that he is in my heart forever and always.

MULTIPLE CHOICE

So, in this final chapter, I ask you to please grab your No. 2 pencil and complete the following. OK, I don't mean literally but you get the point.

AS I READ THIS BOOK, IT MADE ME WANT TO
a) Cry
b) Laugh
c) Buy a copy of the book for every friend I know
d) All of the above

Did you pick D? You chose D, right? C'mon, I mean really, you did, right? Just pretend it's D. Humor me, people. Please, pick D…

You picked D? Oh my gosh, thank you so much!

No, but really.
Thank you.